THE SACRIFICE OF PRAISE

H Bavinck

"The biblical wisdom and deep spirituality of this little book should not be overlooked. What a blessing to have Bavinck's brilliance passed down to us in a new English edition. The translation is elegant, and the historical introduction immensely valuable. Most of all, Bavinck's insights—on everything from sacraments to shame—are edifying in the truest sense of the word. There are lessons here that will help parents, children, educators, pastors, students, new Christians, and seasoned saints. *Sacrifice of Praise* is a gem."

—Kevin DeYoung, Senior Pastor
Christ Covenant Church, Matthews, North Carolina
Assistant Professor of Systematic Theology
Reformed Theological Seminary, Charlotte

"I'm not sure why we (including myself) tend to think that dead theologians have little to say in regard to our current concerns, or that their writing will be dense, difficult to understand, or simply uninteresting. This new translation of Bavinck's *Sacrifice of Praise* is proof to the contrary. Every parent who wonders if their baptized child is genuinely embracing faith should read it. Every parent who doesn't like to do battle in the pew to keep their young child from taking the elements of Communion should read it. But this book's challenge to make confession of faith a continual part of the Christian life is not just about our children; it's for all of us. I found Bavinck's thoroughly readable and warm writing enlightening, challenging, and often moving. This book implanted in me a greater longing for the culmination of human history when all will bow and confess that Jesus is Lord to the glory of God the Father."

—Nancy Guthrie, author and Bible teacher

"In our age—often shallow, distracted, and confused—this book will sound like a thunderclap. It is a classic study on the necessity and centrality of Christ and of how we should learn to think of life, from parenting to worldview, from this center. The perspective is Reformed, and the intent is the church's reformation. It is a study at once rigorous, deep, devout, and pastoral."

—David F. Wells, Distinguished Senior Research Professor
Gordon-Conwell Theological Seminary, South Hamilton

"Bavinck writes with one eye on the grand story of redemption across the canon of Scripture, and another eye on the complex experience of that redemption in the contemporary world. We are all indebted to Clausing and Parker for making Bavinck's short pastoral work on the ongoing experience of redemption accessible for the modern reader. Deep within the human heart is always the temptation to negotiate with God the terms of our relationship to him, rather than affirming that we are to simply and profoundly live into the terms already established by God. The reminder that grace is never earned but must continually be confessed as a 'sacrifice of praise' is as relevant today as it was when Bavinck composed it a century ago."

—Richard Lints
Andrew Mutch Distinguished Professor of Theology
Gordon-Conwell Theological Seminary, South Hamilton

"Herman Bavinck is best known as a dogmatician of great depth and scope. Yet like all of the greatest theologians, his concern for the church cannot be reduced to his scholarly contributions. He also earnestly desired to encourage and nurture other believers in their faith, a fact to which these short addresses give remarkable testimony. In them, he discusses the whole idea of confessing Christ in the various stages of Christian discipleship, from baptism through to the Lord's Supper and beyond. This is practical Reformed piety at its best: rooted in the word, connected to the sacraments, and focused upon Christ."

—Carl R. Trueman
Professor of Biblical and Religious Studies
Grove City College, Pennsylvania

"In Bavinck's own biography, participation in the Lord's Supper was far from inconsequential. As Clausing and Parker note, the student-era Bavinck first took part after extended, careful reflection on the gospel and its fruit in his own life. Having done so, the sacrament proved a regular source of spiritual comfort to him. In The Sacrifice of Praise, we find a set of reflections on the Supper that are richly theological, pastoral, and practical. We owe Clausing and Parker a debt of gratitude for their work in presenting this text to us in a fresh new form."

—James Eglinton, Meldrum Lecturer in Reformed Theology
New College, University of Edinburgh

THE SACRIFICE OF PRAISE

Meditations before and after Admission to the Lord's Supper

By Herman Bavinck

Translated and edited by
Cameron Clausing and Gregory Parker Jr.

Foreword by Scott R. Swain

The Sacrifice of Praise: Meditations before and after Admission to the Lord's Supper

Hendrickson Publishers Marketing, LLC
P. O. Box 3473
Peabody, Massachusetts 01961-3473
www.hendrickson.com

ISBN 978-1-68307-198-3

Printed in the United States of America

Second Printing — January 2020

Library of Congress Cataloging-in-Publication

Names: Bavinck, Herman, 1854-1921, author.
Title: The sacrifice of praise : meditations before and after admission to the Lord's Supper / Bavinck Herman ; translated and edited by Cameron Clausing and Gregory Parker Jr. ; foreword by Scott Swain.
Description: Peabody, MA : Hendrickson Publishers, 2019. | Includes bibliographical references and index.
Identifiers: LCCN 2019001737 | ISBN 9781683071983 (alk. paper)
Subjects: LCSH: Lord's Supper--Meditations. | Theology, Doctrinal--Meditations.
Classification: LCC BV826.5 .B3813 2019 | DDC 264/.36--dc23
LC record available at https://lccn.loc.gov/2019001737

Dedicated to Taryn, Calvin, and Danae

Contents

Foreword

The past several decades have witnessed a renewal of Reformed theology in North America and the United Kingdom. This renewal has been fueled in no small measure by the translation and publication of significant works of Reformed theology in the English language. Among the recently translated works that have enabled a new generation of Christians to retrieve the riches of the Reformed heritage, Herman Bavinck's four-volume *Reformed Dogmatics* holds a distinguished place. Originally published in Dutch at the beginning of the twentieth century, Bavinck's *Reformed Dogmatics* offers today's church a mature statement of Reformed teaching that is comprehensive in scope, conversant with a wide range of ecclesiastical and modern viewpoints, irenic in tone, and doxological in aim.

Unfortunately, the renewal of Reformed theology in recent days has not, in every instance, resulted in a corresponding renewal of Reformed practice and piety. This is a lamentable situation. Though we may be grateful for conferences and websites that celebrate the sovereignty of God and the doctrines of grace, if the renewal of Reformed theology is to beget anything more than a movement, it must find concrete expression in the church's life and ministry. Reformed theology will not flourish in the long run if it does not take root in the church of Jesus Christ. Thankfully, the same strategy for renewing Reformed theology through the publication of classic texts can aid the renewal of Reformed practice and piety. Here too Herman Bavinck has gifts to give.

Herman Bavinck's *The Sacrifice of Praise* is best understood as a work of catechetical theology, suitable for sharing with baptized Christians on the occasion of their public profession of faith and admission to the Lord's Table. The book's focus, as the title suggests, is the Christian duty of confessing Jesus Christ as Lord before God and human beings. This duty, Bavinck argues, is a delightful task, "a sacrifice of praise" (Heb. 13:15) to the Triune God.

The Sacrifice of Praise exhibits many of the virtues that readers have come to appreciate in Bavinck the theologian. Always with an eye focused on the supreme Lordship of the Triune God, and therefore on all that falls within his sovereign domain, Bavinck treats a range of topics whose height and depth span heaven and earth and whose breadth and length span from the beginning and to the end of the world. In each instance, he is mindful of his topic's relation to the Triune God and to the full scope of God's works in creation, redemption, and consummation. Bavinck traces the unfolding administration of God's kingdom in the covenant of redemption, the covenant of works, and the covenant of grace. He expounds God's work of grace and our work of gratitude, ably distinguishing (without dividing) and relating (without confusing) divine and human agency within the covenant of grace. Bavinck describes the act of confessing Jesus as Lord in its various formal and informal, individual and communal contexts, all the while acknowledging the fundamental unity of the Christian confession. In discussing these and other topics, *The Sacrifice of Praise* presents a compelling vision of Christian discipleship as devotion to Jesus as Lord in word and deed, worship and witness.

Even when writing for a popular audience, Bavinck always penetrates to the heart of the topic he addresses. The present topic is no exception. According to Bavinck, confession holds the place it does in the Christian life because of who God is and because of who we are as creatures, made and renewed in his image. From all eternity, God is an eloquent God. The Father eternally utters his Word in the person of his Son. Through his self-same Word and Son, the Father creates, rules, redeems, and perfects all things for the sake of his name. Furthermore, as those created and renewed in God's image, we are eloquent creatures. Speech is the crowning glory of our identity and calling. The image of God shines most clearly in us when we confess with our lips that Jesus is Lord. Our calling as God's vice-regents in the world shines most clearly in us when we summon the rest of God's creatures in heaven and on earth to join us in praising the name of the Lord: "My mouth will speak the praise of the Lord, and let all flesh bless his holy name forever and ever" (Ps. 145:21).

Along with the aforementioned virtues of Bavinck the theologian, this book exhibits the virtues of Bavinck the churchman. Bavinck traces the progress of Christian nurture from baptism through confession to participation in the Lord's Supper, demonstrating the organic relationship that binds the various elements of Christian nurture together. He discusses the relationship between the individual's personal profession of faith and the church's historic confessions, steering a course between an insecure pietism and a cold orthodoxy. He treats the place of parents, schools, and churches in Christian nurture, rightly emphasizing the priority of the word of God among the various means of grace that God has appointed for his people. Alert to the challenges that threaten the Christian's confidence in this vale of tears, Bavinck grounds the security of the Christian's confession in Jesus Christ's faithful confession and inspires the Christian to look with eager expectation to the day when every knee will bow and every tongue will confess that Jesus Christ is Lord to the glory of God the Father.

As the father of four children, I was especially encouraged by the wisdom this book conveys. Our children find themselves at various stages of Christian discipleship and therefore with various needs for instruction and encouragement in the Lord. My youngest child is ready to make his public profession of faith before the church. My oldest child is about to head off to university. In Bavinck's *The Sacrifice of Praise*, I found a treasure trove of resources for instructing and encouraging our children in their various stages of Christian discipleship. I trust that other pastors, teachers, and parents will find this book to be a valuable resource as well.

The Sacrifice of Praise may be profitably read alongside two other books of catechetical theology written by Herman Bavinck. *The Wonderful Works of God* is a compendium of Christian doctrine that clearly and concisely summarizes the main elements of biblical teaching confessed by Reformed churches. *Saved by Grace: The Holy Spirit's Work in Calling and Regeneration* discusses the covenantal basis of infant baptism and addresses questions often debated among Christians regarding the spiritual status of those baptized in infancy. Together, these three books represent a kind of catechetical trilogy that—if widely studied and discussed among pastors, elders, and laypersons—would greatly aid the church in its task of making disciples of Jesus Christ.

The translators and publisher are to be commended for their labors in making a new edition of Bavinck's *The Sacrifice of Praise* available to an English-speaking audience. May this book contribute to a revitalized culture of catechesis in our churches and thereby to the greater flourishing of Reformed theology among all nations to the praise of Jesus' name.

Scott R. Swain, President and
James Woodrow Hassell Professor of Systematic Theology
Reformed Theological Seminary, Orlando, Florida

Acknowledgments

The translation of a book on confessing one's faith before, during, and after the Lord's Supper invokes a special gratitude toward our families and the faithful preaching of the gospel by the ministers who led us to our own confession of faith. In God's sovereignty and grace, we are indebted to Rev. Mark Evans and Rev. Dr. George Grant. The endeavor to complete a new translation of Bavinck's *The Sacrifice of Praise* is a testimony to your faithfulness to the Lord and his people.

We would like to thank Dr. Dolf te Velde and Dr. James Eglinton for their generosity and enthusiasm for the project. Both provided help in clarifying the meaning of several archaic Dutch idioms and were a wealth of historical knowledge. Their willingness to help has modeled much of what it means to be a scholar for us.

We are also thankful to Andrew Keenan, Dr. Zachary Purvis, Dr. Bruce Pass, Dr. Adonis Vidu, Rev. Timothy Wheeler, and Dr. Takayuki Yagi for their friendship, encouragement, and steady inquiries into the state of the project, which played a role in its progression toward completion. The publication would not have been possible without our publishing friends, the staff at Hendrickson Publishers, who were adept at turning the toil of our labor into a fruit for the church—moreover, whose kindness toward us will not soon be forgotten. We are also grateful for the support of our churches and countless individuals for their financial and spiritual support during our studies, the list of whom would stretch the margins of this book. Your partnership with us in the gospel is a beautifully intimate illustration of the parable of the talents.

Above all, this work would not have seen the light of day if not for the love, encouragement, and patience of Taryn, Calvin, and Danae, to whom this book is dedicated.

Soli Deo Gloria
Cameron Clausing
Gregory Parker Jr.
Edinburgh, Scotland

Introduction

The importance of confessing the faith can be seen from the earliest days of the church to the present. On the occasion of Peter's confession that Jesus was the Christ, Jesus said to him:

> "Blessed are you, Simon Bar-Jonah! For flesh and blood has not revealed this to you, but my Father who is in heaven. And I tell you, you are Peter, and on this rock I will build my church, and the gates of hell shall not prevail against it. I will give you the keys of the kingdom of heaven, and whatever you bind on earth shall be bound in heaven, and whatever you loose on earth shall be loosed in heaven."
>
> (Matt. 16:17–19)

In Acts 7, when Stephen made a public confession of who Jesus is, what he has done, and what he is doing, he was stoned to death. In the early church account of the martyrdom of Polycarp, when Polycarp was called on to recant his confession of Christ, he said, "Eighty and six years have I served Him, and He never did me any injury: how then can I blaspheme my King and my Savior?"[1] The split in the church that prompted Augustine to write *On Baptism, Against the Donatist* dealt in part with the question surrounding those who recant their faith in the face of persecution but later return to the church. The works of those—and others, such as Anselm, Aquinas, and Bonaventure—are works of public confession of the person and work of Christ. The reform movements of the Waldensians, Wycliffe, and Hus were all efforts to both purify and call for a faithful confession of faith, and the Reformation was in large part a call for and a test of the Reformers' confessions of faith. The list could go on. Church history is replete with examples of the importance of regular, public, and faithful confessions of faith.

This new translation of the work by Dutch theologian Herman Bavinck (1854–1921) is a call to this historic Christian practice. Bavinck wrote it originally for people in the Netherlands who had been baptized and were ready to make a public confession of faith. After they had done this and received the Lord's Supper for the first time, it was customary to give them a book. At the turn of the twentieth century, *The Sacrifice of Praise* was among the most popular gifts. Bavinck wrote it as a reminder that confession of the faith is necessary, not only at conversion but in all of life, in words and in deeds. It was written to encourage and challenge them toward a deeper reflection of the nature of their confession. It was written to educate and comfort. It was written as a thoughtful theological work, but also as a tender pastoral hand leading the young Christian further up and further into the beauty of Christ and the gospel. It was written to tether the reader to Scripture and to the rest of the church.

The Sacrifice of Praise: A New Translation

In 1921, John Dolfin (pastor of Bethany Reformed Christian Church in Muskegon, Michigan) first translated Herman Bavinck's *De Offerande des Lofs* into *The Sacrifice of Praise* (*SoP*). This raises the question as to why, if there is already an English translation of this work, would anyone want to undertake a new translation? There are multiple reasons.

First, we believe that at times Dolfin took certain translation liberties with which we disagree—such as blunting the more modern features of Bavinck's writing or adding and dropping sentence clauses, and in some cases dropping whole paragraphs.[2] We desired to bring to the contemporary reader a version of *SoP* that retains Bavinck's distinctive style and expression—while being cognizant of our own context and audience and therefore restricting ourselves from more dynamic renderings. We wanted Bavinck to speak to us today, and our hope is that this new translation does just that.

Second, we thought the use of modern language was fitting as current-day readers are no longer as accustomed to the older King James English. In addition to this, as one reads through *SoP*, it becomes apparent that the book is replete with scriptural reference, quotations, and allusions that were unattributed. We desired to make these biblical allusions, quotations, and paraphrases explicit. Therefore, we thought it prudent to use a contemporary translation of Scripture. We utilized the English Standard Version (ESV) of the Bible for our translation. Although Bavinck's original text does not provide scriptural citations, we decided that adding this would aid the reader. Additionally, we include editorial endnotes to guide the reader through this "ripe fruit placed in the bosom of the church." Also, where suitable, we utilized language that would allow for a more inclusive reading, while not obscuring Bavinck's meaning or making the language overly cumbersome.

Third, for many years, theologians have praised Herman Bavinck for his richly scriptural, highly Trinitarian, Christocentric, confessional, modern, and perspicuous theology. International admiration for Bavinck as a theologian started long before his introduction to the Anglophone world. Writing to a friend in 1924, Swiss-German theologian Karl Barth said that Bavinck was a theologian with class; and in his *Göttingen Dogmatics*, Barth writes that Bavinck's presentation of the Trinity was one of the most careful and instructive that he knew.[3] Likewise, Dutch Reformed theologian Cornelius Van Til heralded Bavinck's *Gereformeerde Dogmatiek* as "the greatest and most comprehensive statement of Reformed systematic theology in modern times."[4] Similarly, French Protestant theologian Auguste Lecerf deemed the work as "a veritable *summa* of contemporary Calvinism."[5]

Since the English inception of Bavinck's *Reformed Dogmatics*, praise of and interest in Bavinck have grown significantly. In recent years, a wider community has begun engaging Bavinck and including him among the list of giants in the Reformed tradition.[6] One of these is Tim Keller, the founding pastor of Redeemer Presbyterian Church in New York, who was recently listed as one of the twelve most effective preachers in the English world. In a recent interview,

Keller attributed Bavinck's "grace restores nature" theme as fundamental to his own theology and vision for Redeemer Presbyterian.[7]

While Bavinck's recognition as a theologian will and should continue to receive attention, Bavinck as a theologian-pastor or a churchly dogmatician has been underplayed. Bavinck consciously performed his theological task with the church in mind. Select works, such as James Eglinton's *Herman Bavinck on Preaching and Preachers* (Hendrickson, 2017), have drawn attention to this aspect of Bavinck. Accordingly, *SoP* exists to continue to cultivate this vision of Bavinck as an ecclesial theologian amid this renaissance of interest in him.

In 1881, Bavinck addressed the Central Pastoral Conference in Utrecht. In his presentation, he laid out three methodological considerations for dogmatics. First, dogmatics is always ecclesial and therefore confessional.[8] By this, Bavinck wanted listeners to recognize that theology is not "a private opinion or individual sentiment," nor strictly "biblical," for this would result in a system that most likely has "anti-ecclesiastical impulses . . . and . . . compel(s) all ecclesiastical differences to the same level, committing an offense against its own existence and history."[9] Rather, theology is the "faith truth declared and confessed" by the "whole church or by one of its branches."[10] Second, theology is not the task of an individual or of private opinion, but rather an authorized church teaching in which the whole community of saints participates. Theology is an ecclesial act; it is church based.

Ten years later in 1891, Bavinck wrote a short paper titled "Confession and Dogmatics," reflecting on a presentation and book under the same name by Reformed theologian and preacher François Daubanton.[11] Bavinck writes:

> The dogmatist cannot break free from his past, from his bondage to the community of the church, in which he was born and raised. Every dogmatics can be viewed through the church to which the writer belongs and the confession which led him to Scripture. Christian may be the name, but every dogmatist has a nickname.[12] . . . Jesus has promised to his church the guidance of the Holy Spirit into all truth.

> This is the Church Doctor. And the church is not just an assembly, but also the mother of believers, a mother also of the theologian and the dogmatist. Through her he was led to the truth in Christ. From her hand he received the bread of life. She also was the pillar and firmness of truth for him.

In the same letter, Bavinck discusses the work of the theologian as contributing to the perpetuation of a healthy church:

> [The theologian] must recapitulate the work of the church, as it were, to develop the dogmatics for our eyes from the Scriptures, and to produce it anew. Through this he will to no small degree contribute to the preservation of the church and confession from petrification and dead orthodoxy. For he takes the dogma and dips it into the fresh bath of the water of life, time and time again, where there is the rushing of water in the Holy Scriptures.[13]

Finally, we also included a translation of well-known Dutch preacher William Gispen's review of *SoP* as an epilogue to the book. This provides the reader with a historical looking glass of the book's reception in the Netherlands. In 1901, a small publishing house in The Hague, Fred. H. Verschoor, first published *The Sacrifice of Praise*.[14] Between 1901 and 1906, the book went through four editions, with the second print run occurring just four weeks after the first—which Bavinck notes in his preface to the second edition as having exceeded his expectation. In 1907, J. C. de Mildt (also in The Hague) published the fifth edition, which includes Bavinck's second preface. In 1911, J. H. Kok in Kampen published the sixth edition, with the seventh to tenth editions running between 1912 and 1920.

The 1920 edition of *De Offerande des Lofs* was the version used for this translation. The average print run estimated by J. H. Kok was between 2,000 and 3,000 copies, with the book experiencing at least sixteen reprints, the last of which was in 1948. These numbers suggest that around 40,000 copies of the book circulated throughout the Netherlands during the twentieth century. Gispen's review, which was published less than a month after the initial distribution of *SoP*, writes highly of Bavinck's contribution to church. He says that *SoP* is not "a dogmatic writing, but all the dogmas that are hidden in God's word, in so far as they relate directly to the man's salvation and living unto God's honor, compose the bones of these meditations. And these are not the dry bones of a mounted skeleton, but rather they are bones of a living organism full of fat and marrow." To that end, we retranslated Bavinck's *SoP* for the next generation in a language that is more familiar, and with scriptural citations, so that Bavinck can be heard once more to a modern audience.

The Sacrifice of Praise: Historical Background

The Sacrifice of Praise was written during a fascinating time in Dutch history. It has as its backdrop the faithful secession of two Dutch church groups and the union of two historic giants in Abraham Kuyper (1837–1920) and Bavinck. In the midst of this union, however, there is also controversy, and Bavinck writes this popular-level book as part of his response to the dilemma. In order to situate the place of the book within this history, it is necessary for the whole story to be unfolded, starting with Bavinck himself. This will give the reader an idea of not only the historical significance of the book but also a succinct introduction to its content and the theologian behind it.

Born into the home of a Dutch secessionist preacher in 1854, Herman, along with his six siblings, was shaped by the rhythms of a home steeped in the word of God and the Three Forms of Unity (the confessional commitments of the continental Calvinist churches: the Belgic Confession, the Canons of Dort, and the Heidelberg Catechism) that colored the *Afscheiding* (secessionist) churches. On Wednesday, March 19, 1873, at a midweek catechism class, Bavinck gave a profession of faith at the age of eighteen and was confirmed one Sunday later by Rev. Dosker.[15] In his teenage diary, Bavinck does not reflect on the event; rather, it seems that this profession of faith was more of a matter of thinking through the confessional standards of the church and agreeing with them. It is after one's profession of faith that one is encouraged to search one's heart.

Thus Bavinck entered a time of anxious consideration regarding the motives and intentions of his own soul. It is also during this time that Bavinck began studying at the *Christelijke Gereformeerde Kerken* (Christian Reformed Church) Theological School in Kampen, and a year later he continued his university education in Leiden. From 1874 to 1880, Bavinck studied under the scientific model of professors; and although he admired their approach, he found himself in deep disagreement with them. In Leiden, when Bavinck was twenty, he participated in the Lord's Supper for the first time. In his diary entry of October 10, 1875, Bavinck writes,

> Rev. Donner spoke about Ps. 34:9. It was the Lord's Supper. For the first in my life I expressed at the table of the Lord the public profession that I am dead in sins and misdeeds, but my only hope is on the righteousness of Christ. O may I not have eaten and drunken judgment upon myself! Let, O God, the wish to serve you have been a true one, and thus, an irrevocable one![16]

It is interesting to note that nine hundred and twenty-four days pass between Bavinck's profession of faith and his partaking of the Lord's Supper. The time between his confession of faith and the Lord's Supper should not be seen as a period when he questioned his faith or the tenets of Christianity. Rather, it was a normal part of secessionist piety, in which it was expected that the believer would search his heart. The fact that this happened while Bavinck was in Leiden is significant, for many have suggested that while Bavinck was there, he questioned his orthodox faith. On the other hand, however, the exact opposite appears to be true. Bavinck not only grew in his faith but also took an "irrevocable" step forward. Following the completion of his doctorate at Leiden, Bavinck returned home for a year before entering the pastorate, where he remained for another year before receiving a call to teach at Kampen in 1882, where he then taught from 1883 to 1901. It was at Kampen that he wrote his magnum opus *Gereformeerde Dogmatiek* (*Reformed Dogmatics*).

In certain ways, *SoP* is particularly poignant for people in this time of life. It addresses those who have been baptized and are now journeying toward confession of faith and the Lord's Supper—those who are between the acknowledgement of the head and the relinquishing of the heart. This is why the original subtitle of this book is *Meditations before and after Admission to the Lord's Supper*, which places it within the context of the Lord's Supper. Nonetheless, as Bavinck works out the nature of confession, the book is applicable for the whole of the Christian walk.

A rising star in Dutch society during this time, Abraham Kuyper, founded the *Vrije Universiteit Amsterdam* (Free University of Amsterdam) in 1880. A year later, Kuyper recognized Bavinck's talent as a dogmatician, and he attempted to recruit him to his Free University. He failed in this first attempt, in part because he wanted Bavinck to teach Semitic languages instead of dogmatics. While the two would not work together in a church setting until over a decade later, they had a mutual influence on each other and the wider theological movements occurring in the Netherlands at the time. One historian has said,

> When mentioned together, we take the names of Abraham Kuyper and Herman Bavinck not as the name of two individuals but as a brand name. Kuyper and Bavinck belong together like Goldman and Sachs or Mercedes and Benz. Together they stand for neo-Calvinism.[17]

To understand the historical context that lead to the writing of *SoP*, it is necessary to briefly explore the history of the *De Gereformeerde Kerken in Nederland* (*GKN*).

The Break from the Dutch National Church

In 1892, Herman Bavinck and Abraham Kuyper forged a partnership when they brought together two distinct reform movements—the *Afscheiding* (founded in 1834) and the *Doleantie* (founded in 1886)—as the *De Gereformeerde Kerken in Nederland* (*GKN*).[18]

The *Afscheiding*, or Churches of the Secession, started as an attempt to reform the national church, but it became a denomination in its own right when the reforms were rejected. In its early years, a pastor from Ulrum, Hendrik de Cock, led the movement that focused mainly on the recovery of the historic documents on which the Reformed Church was founded.[19] De Cock, and those who followed him, had perceived a subtle erosion to the doctrinal standards of the church through the influence of the Enlightenment, and so they ended up leaving the national church. The first years of the split were difficult, and the *Afscheiding* experienced much persecution.[20] However, through the work of Groen van Prinsterer, a Dutch politician, and his defense of their right of secession, the secessionists experienced something of a respite. The persecution began to decline even further in 1840 when William II succeeded his father as king, finally subsiding with the new constitution in 1848, which granted freedom of religion.[21] In 1854, this allowed the young church to organize and found its own theological school in Kampen; and in 1882, Herman Bavinck was appointed professor of dogmatics.

The history of the *Doleantie* (the Churches of the Grieving), a group of churches ejected from the Dutch Reformed Church in 1886, is much different.[22] Organized under the leadership of Abraham Kuyper,[23] it was a failed attempt to reform the Dutch Reformed Church from liberalism. Unlike the *Afscheiding*, since the prospects for their proposed reforms seemed more and more remote, Kuyper instead founded the Free University of Amsterdam in 1880. This was one of a number of steps toward an independently organized Reformed orthodoxy.[24] The conflict between Kuyper and his followers, and the rest of the national church, came to head when Kuyper and a coalition of pastors refused to receive progressive catechumens as members. The regional governing ecclesiastical body directed them to do so; when they refused, the authorities suspended eighty office bearers in Amsterdam from ministry. By the end of the year, Kuyper was among those who had been deposed. In 1886, Kuyper and others began this new assembly of churches known as the *Doleantie*.[25]

In 1892, after several years of debate, the two groups that had seceded from the Dutch Reformed church merged and became the *GKN* (*De Gereformeerde Kerken in Nederland*), with Kuyper on one side and Bavinck on the other. Even with Kuyper and Bavinck backing the union, however, there was still some suspicion on both sides, which caused some members of the earlier secessionist group to continue as the *Christelijke Gereformeerde Kerk* (Christian Reformed Church).[26] Although the churches that remained in the *GKN* moved forward, within a decade, some of Kuyper's particular theological positions began to produce discord in the *GKN*.

A Difference of Opinions

In 1905, three years after Bavinck transitioned from Kampen to Amsterdam after accepting Kuyper's plea to teach theology at the Free University, the *GKN* Synod in Utrecht adjudicated theological disagreements that had finally reached a boiling point.—the main controversy being Kuyper's views on regeneration and baptism.[27] In a series of articles originally published from March 1901 to May 1902 in the Dutch religious newspaper *De Bazuin*, Bavinck entered the debate, and in 1903 he published his book *Roeping en Wedergeboorte* (*Calling and Regeneration*).[28]

Kuyper's peculiar positions encompassed four particular areas: (1) supralapsarianism versus infralapsarianism;[29] (2) justification from eternity; (3) immediate regeneration; and (4) presumptive regeneration.[30] (Since Bavinck primarily engages the last category in *The Sacrifice of Praise*, we will focus only on that point here.) The question that needed to be answered in Bavinck's day regarded the status of children of believing parents. Kuyper's tendency was to start from standpoint of election and assume that a child possessed God's grace in Christ, just as the sacrament of baptism both signified and sealed.[31] His logic says that because the promise of God is given only to the elect, it should be assumed that those who are baptized possess all of the benefits promised in baptism.[32] Kuyper's main concerns in formulating this theological understanding regarded "religious formalism," where one would have congregations full of baptized yet unsaved people, and "Reformed pietism," which demanded conversion experiences as proof of person's salvation.[33]

Before proceeding too much further here, we want to make it clear that Kuyper's position was not an attempt to make presumptions about what God had decreed about certain individuals. Rather, Kuyper was primarily concerned with the attitude of the church toward its covenant children. Kuyper was not attempting to make a statement about a baptized person's status as regenerate; he was arguing for a particular stance that the church and believing parents should take toward a covenant child in light of the promises of God in Scripture. He claimed that this was based on the divine promise and that God was already at work efficaciously to save the child. The church should therefore administer baptism to the child based on this assumption, and then watch over time for that faith to work itself out in open profession and repentance. Kuyper writes,

> You certainly now know that my child is chosen, and God has already wrought in this child the secret seed of regeneration. Then, naturally, you could not withhold holy baptism from your child. On this ground it is your duty. As much as you live in the covenant, each of your children, who were born to you, on the assumption that the work of God's grace already grabbed a place in them, must be baptized in the Triune name of God.[34]

While Bavinck is careful not to mention Kuyper directly in his treatment on baptism, regeneration, faith, and repentance, Bavinck's language is clearly a break from Kuyper's argument. Unlike Kuyper, Bavinck considered the covenant of grace as the foundation for baptism:[35]

> Not regeneration, faith, or repentance, much less our assumption pertaining to them, but only the covenant of grace gave people, both adults and children, the right to baptism. This covenant was the sure, scriptural, objective ground upon which all the Reformed, together and without distinction, based the right to infant baptism. They had no other, deeper, or more solid ground.[36]

Bavinck's argument that the grounding for baptism finds it surest footing in the covenant of grace and not election does not mean he does not call for the church to show charity in its judgment of children. Indeed, he asserts that it is impossible to make an "infallible pronouncement that establishes the salvation of every person." However, the "basis for baptism is not the assumption that someone is regenerate, nor even that [there is] regeneration itself, but only the covenant of God."[37]

Bavinck's concern regarding "assumed" or "presumptive" regeneration was a pastoral one. He argued that while the doctrine provided no practical benefit, it did lend itself to inflicting much spiritual harm. To be fair, Bavinck did not believe that it necessarily led to harm but that it could easily do this. Bavinck argued that three harms were induced from Kuyper's position. First, it ran the risk of lulling the baptized into a false sense of security. Second, the gospel is preached to and for the regenerate; others need only profess their reprobation. Third, the teaching leads to an understanding of the gospel that is out of accord with the Scriptures and Reformed standards.[38]

The "Conclusions of Utrecht"

In 1905, this divergence in the understanding of baptism, regeneration, repentance, and covenant caused such a disturbance in the church that the Synod Utrecht presented its "Conclusions" to settle the matter for the *GKN*. In the end, the actual distance between Kuyper's and Bavinck's positions on "presumptive" regeneration was small. (Bavinck's "judgment of charity" concerning covenant children was similar to that of Kuyper's understanding that position, vis-à-vis the posture of the church and believing parents toward their children.) The deep disagreement was in the grounding of baptism in this assumption of regeneration. Bavinck held that the basis for baptism was found solely in God's covenant of grace. As Bavinck saw it, Kuyper's position made a human response to God's promise for baptism. While the 1905 "Conclusions of Utrecht" confirm Bavinck's reasoning over Kuyper's,[39] they were not an attempt to be polemic but rather a mediating document that attempts a compromise to pacify the conflict that had arisen in the *GKN*. Nevertheless, Kuyper's views were met with moderate condemnation.

The Sacrifice of Praise: A Summary

It was in the midst of the heat of this controversy that Bavinck wrote *The Sacrifice of Praise*.[40] While not an overt polemic against Kuyper and his positions concerning baptism, covenant, faith, repentance, and the need for a public confession of faith, this book was the presentation of a position incongruous with Kuyper's. Bavinck held that the theme of confession that needs to be made—before, on, and after receiving admission to the Lord's Supper—is seen both as a scriptural mandate and as an antidote against many of the dangers Bavinck saw inherent in Kuyper's position of assumed regeneration.

For Bavinck, confessing the faith with a view of the covenant, regeneration, faith, and repentance in line with the historic creeds and confessions provided great benefit and guarded against the inherent harm he perceived from assumed regeneration. First, properly understood, a public confession of faith would keep the believer from being lulled into a false sense of security. As Bavinck lays out in *SoP*, a public confession of faith calls believers to a life of repentance and faith—to deny themselves, take up their cross, and follow Christ.

Second, in *SoP* Bavinck shows that the confession of faith is not reserved to a limited few but that Scripture calls all to this confession. From a human perspective, a person's final status is determined not at birth but at death. The duty of the church is to call the whole world to make this confession of faith, not just the baptized few. Among Bavinck's concerns in *SoP* is to show that all are called to confession, and therefore the preaching of the gospel is not solely for believers but is intended for the whole world.

Lastly, Bavinck's concern in *SoP* is to show that this call for all people everywhere to make public confession is in line not just with the historic Reformed tradition but with all of Scripture. The need to confess the faith is mandated throughout the Bible, in both the Old Testament and the New Testament. Here, Bavinck calls on Christians to see it as their duty to regularly make a credible confession of faith in word and deed. Indeed, the confession of faith is not a one-time event but a regular and continual part of the Christian life.

In the first chapter, Bavinck takes a wide theological scope, introducing us to the covenants of redemption, works, and grace. He assures us that salvation is only by grace as it is cemented in the eternal covenant of God, and that the sacraments are signs and seals of the promises made to believers through these covenants. Likewise, the believer's own confession of faith is rooted in God's eternal divine mercy. Having introduced us to confession as an act of covenantal grace toward believers, Bavinck moves in the second chapter to the believer's participation in the covenant of grace. In this covenant, believers have the blessed and beautiful responsibility to actively train children in the task of being transformed to radiantly reflect the divine image of God that they have received. In this chapter, Bavinck suggests that there are three avenues that assist in this "building up" process: family, church, and school.

In the third chapter, having discussed where this "building up" activity takes place, he now contends for the primacy of the Scripture in the task of "building up." He argues that since piety and orthodoxy must not be torn asunder, instruction in doctrine and theology must be accompanied by training in life. Therefore, word and deed, life and doctrine, walk and talk are joined together. He says that the Word may come to believers not just in the sermon or the private reading of Scripture, but that it is with them on all paths as they live in full dependence on the Word.

In the fourth chapter, Bavinck describes the true nature of confession—that it is not simply spoken but embodied. It is done "with mouth and heart, word and deed." Confession is the lived, daily profession of faith that bears fruit in every sphere of life. The whole life of one who professes faith is "inseparable from the faith of the heart"; it is a confession of praise before God.

In chapter five, Bavinck contends that confession is twofold. First, confession is repentance, a declaration of one's sin and guilt before God. Second, confession is the profession of dependence on the person of Jesus Christ, whose life, death, and resurrection constitute the essence of Christianity.

In chapter six, Bavinck considers the diversity of confession present in the church across the ages. He acknowledges that while this diversity has caused damage to the church, it may also reflect the great work of God in re-creation. As God is a trinity, but also unity in diversity, so is this diversity reflected in his organic creation. Likewise, God's act of recreation does not oppose the creation's inherent diversity. Rather, in the diversity of believers, they are united in Christ.

Building on this, in chapter seven Bavinck explains how this superlative diversity of confession finds its unity in the common confession of Christ as Lord. Here he then articulates the absoluteness of Christianity, both its exclusivity (that it denies the truthfulness of all other religions) and in its inclusiveness (that in this declaration of the Lordship of Christ, the universal, international church possesses unity). In the unity of this confession, the universality of Christianity is implied.

In chapter eight, Bavinck turns to consider the duty or obligation of the believer to confess the faith. He first discusses how God, who eternally self-communicates his word, at the same time, is the self-speaking Word toward his creation: his creation was spoken into existence and is preserved by the same Word. Likewise, the image of God is called to speak, to profess in spoken word, the great name of the Lord. In this confession, the fruit of our lips is the sacrifice of praise, which belongs both to the individual and the community of believers—the fruit of the tree and the orchard.

In chapter nine, Bavinck addresses that which opposes professions of faith: the flesh, the world, and the devil. He writes first positively of the shame that comes from sin, which he sees as a healthy guilt that leads us back to God. However, there is also a false shame, which the principalities of darkness thrust upon believers. False shame is the embarrassment of professing Christ as Lord and Savior. Bavinck encourages believers to fight against this second kind of shame, which wants us to root our lives in the appearance of being rich and enriched. Rather, we should recognize that Christ himself became this shame on our behalf, and that in identifying with him we are lifted up with him. In confession, then, we profess that we have nothing apart from Christ. At the same time, this confession unites us to Christ, the one who welcomes us as fellow heirs and who removes our shame.

In the tenth chapter, Bavinck reminds believers that they are never alone when they confess Christ. They stand with the saints of the past, the hosts of heaven, the church of today, and Christ himself. Moreover, the Father and the Son sent the Spirit to work in each of them, bringing them to a confession of Christ. Thus confessors of Christ are never alone, for they are in eternal fellowship with God.

In chapter eleven, Bavinck transitions to consider the reward for one's faithful confession. He returns to the covenant of grace, in which it is God alone who destines man to be with him—not by any act of man. We can only passively receive grace from God in faith. Bavinck also exhorts believers to actively pursue their sanctification. In other words, believers should strive to become more of who they are already in Christ. Here we encounter a paradoxical reality of life in Christ: that the unmerited reward of eternal life, which was always the believer's in Christ as a gift, becomes the believer's through perseverance and love. Ultimately, in union with Christ, all of God's children will fellowship with him and enjoy his presence as a reward.

In his final chapter, Bavinck encourages believers with the knowledge that the history of the world ends in the unity of confession that Jesus Christ is Lord. Bavinck contends that while this confession may be opposed in the present, believers can nonetheless take comfort in the hope that the Lord will one day return to judge the living and the dead, that all of creation will fall on its knees before Jesus. Thus in confession we participate at once in an event that was promised and accomplished in the past, guaranteed in eternity, and that one day will be ours in the future forever.

Conclusion

In updating this book, we hope that it edifies the church and helps strengthen Christians everywhere, as it testifies of God's promises, love, and the importance of confession. Our hope is that in a time when the world, the flesh, and the devil press in on all sides, this book functions as a call from the past to make a confession of the faith in the present. Our hope is that this book encourages both young and old, men and women, the trained and the untrained to make a regular, faithful, and true confession of Christ as Lord of heaven and earth. Our hope is that even when we inevitably fail in our calling to confess the name of Christ, Bavinck helps us remember that our Savior remains faithful in confessing our name before the Father, which is the great hope of our confession.

Through him then let us continually offer up a sacrifice of praise to God, that is, the fruit of lips that acknowledge his name. (Heb. 13:15)

THE SACRIFICE OF PRAISE

Meditations before and after Admission to the Lord's Supper

Foreword to the Second Dutch Edition

The favorable reception which accompanied these meditations on before and after admission to the Holy Supper far exceeded the expectation of the writer and publisher. Within four weeks, the initial large print run was sold out. Now a new edition appears, which is a modest version and at a low price, but the content has not undergone any change.

Readers have reported with a unified voice that they immediately understood the title of these meditations was borrowed from Hebrews 13:15. Just as the apostle stirred his fellow Christians on, "Let us continually offer to God a sacrifice of praise—the fruit of the lips that confess his name." In honor of the pious saints of the Old Testament, who when bringing their sacrifices were bound to appointed times, the believers of the New Testament have the invaluable privilege to offer their sacrifice to God at all times. They may do so because they bring this sacrifice through Christ, who by his one perfect sacrifice sanctified and qualified all his people. And they may continually offer their sacrifices because they no longer exist in the slaughter of animals and the pouring of blood, but in giving worship and thanks to God for the abundant blessings which he bestowed upon them in Christ. Their life should therefore be a continuing sacrifice of praise, existing in confession of the name of the Lord.

May these meditations be made useful to many by the Spirit of the Lord!

H. BAVINCK
Kampen, 1901

Preface to the Fifth Dutch Edition

The fifth edition of these meditations was carefully revised, and it increased a little here and there. The material, which was included in the previous edition in the second chapter, was elaborated on and expanded so that it is now split into two chapters, although the substance and scope of the book underwent no change.

H. BAVINCK
Amsterdam, 1907

1

The Foundation of Confession

"And I will establish my covenant between me and you and your offspring after you throughout their generations for an everlasting covenant, to be God to you and to your offspring after you." (Gen. 17:7)

The covenant of grace lies immovably firm and fast in God's eternal mercies.

In the first covenant, which was established prior to the Fall, God came to man with the demand of perfect obedience. He promised man eternal life and heavenly salvation, but only after man perfectly fulfilled the law. This covenant, therefore, dealt with the will and with the work of man; it rested partly in his hand and was thus unstable and breakable.[1]

But the covenant of grace, which was announced for the first time in the maternal promise [see Gen. 3:15], has its basis and security solely in God's gracious counsel. Although the word *covenant* does not appear in this promise, the concept of covenant is fully understood. For before man entered into a covenant of friendship with Satan through his sin, God stepped between them, substituting enmity for friendship, and through the seed of the woman bringing man back to his side. The covenant of grace, therefore, proceeds entirely from God. God himself brings it about. Therefore, it does not rest in man nor is it dependent on his approval. It is eternal, unchangeable, immovable—as is God himself. "'For the mountains may depart and the hills be removed, but my steadfast love shall not depart from you, and my covenant of my peace shall not be removed,' says the LORD, who has compassion on you" [Isa. 54:10].

In this covenant, God is the First and the Last, the Beginning and the End, the Alpha and the Omega [Rev. 22:13]. In the most beautiful way, it maintains the absolute sovereignty of God in the whole work of salvation. For from the very beginning to the very end, nothing of man is added or introduced. Redemption is the divine work par excellence, the work of the Father, the Son, and the Holy Spirit. All boasting is excluded, the glory is entirely and only due to God, who is not only the Creator but also the re-creator of all things.

Therefore, it is a covenant of grace, of pure grace. This covenant has its origins in divine grace, it has its contents in the gift of grace, and its ultimate goal is the glorification of grace. It is God who has established this well-ordered and eternal covenant. It is God who receives man estranged from him by sin. It is God who makes man share in all the benefits of the covenant, who makes man walk in the ways of the covenant, and through this covenant leads him to heavenly blessing.

The surety of this covenant is the reason why in Holy Scripture it is depicted several times as a testament or will. It is not a mutual treaty; it is not the same as an agreement between two persons who, after thinking about and weighing the factors, are able to establish agreement and mutual consent. But the covenant of grace is an institution, a gracious disposition of God, a gift in Christ. "And I assign to you, as my Father assigned to me, a kingdom" [Luke 22:29].

Like with a will or testament, the divine blessings of this covenant come to us as a last free decree in the form of an inheritance and without our volition. It is the most precious gift, the most perfect gift that comes to us "from above, coming down from the Father of lights, with whom there is no variation or shadow due to change" [James 1:17].

And see what kind of blessings make up the contents of this free and eternal covenant. Together they form a fullness of spiritual and material, of heavenly and earthly, of eternal and temporal blessings. In that covenant, there is opened and unlocked for man a fullness of salvation, a fountain of blessedness, a spring of life. One grace segues to another, and that one is replaced by a new grace. Out of the fullness of Christ, we receive grace upon grace [John 1:16].

The benefits that are gifted to the person in this covenant are principally spiritual. Before all else, Christ came to earth to seek and to save the lost [Luke 19:10]. He did not act as a social reformer, as a political leader of the people, as an artist or a philosopher. But Savior was his name and his office. For that, the Father anointed him with his Spirit to bring good tidings to the meek, to bind up the brokenhearted, to proclaim freedom to the captives and the opening of the prison to those who are bound, and to proclaim the year of the Lord's pleasure [Isa. 61:1–2].

Therefore, above all, the Father of our Lord Jesus Christ in heaven blesses the church with spiritual blessings. In union with Christ, forgiveness and regeneration, faith and conversion, sanctification and perseverance become the portion of believers. Both their consciousness and their being, their state and status, are renewed by the Spirit of Christ. They have become different people through the Spirit that dwells in them; they are not from below but from above; they have been born of God, adopted by him as children, and are destined for the heavenly inheritance. For them, "the old has passed away; behold, the new has come" [2 Cor. 5:17].

But these spiritual and eternal blessings are also accompanied by earthly and temporal blessings. Indeed, heaven and earth, spirit and matter, and soul and body so closely depend on each other that an absolute separation is impossible. In the glorious picture of the future that the prophecy of the Old Testament revealed, we not only see that Israel will be a holy nation, which the Lord himself has betrothed in eternity, but the promise is also formulated: that Israel will live in safety under the Prince of Peace who comes out of the House of David, and Israel will enjoy an unprecedented prosperity and extraordinary fruitfulness of the earth [Ezek. 36:36; Isa. 9:6].

Therefore, the New Testament also unites the physical with the spiritual blessings. Certainly, the emphasis falls upon the latter. The kingdom of God with his righteousness must be sought foremost, and that kingdom, already here on earth, becomes the portion for those who believe the gospel of Christ and with their heart turn to

God. For, in the first place, the kingdom is established in the heart and does not consist in food and drink, but in righteousness, joy, and peace through the Holy Spirit.

Whoever has sought after and found the kingdom as a pearl of great price then also receives all other things. Such a person no longer needs to be concerned, like the Gentiles, and ask anxiously: "What will we eat?" or, "What will we drink?" or, "With what will we be clothed?" For his heavenly Father knows that he needs all of these things [Matt. 6:31–32]. He who spared not his own Son, but delivered him up for the guilty, will also with him grant us all things [Rom. 8:32]. The hairs of our heads are all known [Luke 12:7]. Our bread is certain and our water sure [Matt. 6:31–32]. Whoever would follow Jesus must forsake everything [Luke 14:27–28]. Yet even now, in this life, he already receives again fathers and mothers, brothers and sisters, friends and fields, and still in the next age, eternal life [Matt. 19:29]. Godliness with contentment is therefore a great gain; it is useful for all things, having the promise of both for this life and the life to come [Phil. 4:10–13].

All of these benefits of the covenant are summed up in the one great promise: that God will be our God and the God of our seed [Gen. 17:7; Ps. 48:14]. The announcement of salvation begins with this promise, when God, after the Fall, once more seeks man. God breaks the friendship with Satan that was made and, setting enmity in its place, once again includes man into his communion. This promise stands at the head of the covenant that was established with Abraham. It shines above the law given to Israel and forms the main contents of the administration of the covenant of grace in the days of the Old Testament. In that promise, Christians find, amid distress and misery, their salvation and comfort; besides God, they have no one in heaven and on earth they desire nothing but him. He is the strength of their heart and their portion forever [Ps. 73:25–26]. When Israel abandons him, this comfort still remains: that God is still their God, and he again gathers them out of the dispersion; and at the end of days, he establishes a new covenant with them in which they will be his people and he will be their God [Jer. 30:22; 31:31; Rev. 21:3].

And this promise passes over into the New Testament. It is fulfilled in Christ, who—in the most fearful trials, in the severest temptations, in the struggle of Gethsemane, and in the suffering on the cross—remained upright because God was his God and he was God's much loved Son [Matt. 17:5]. It is being fulfilled in the church, which has taken the place of Israel, glorying in the Immanuel, God with us, having been adopted as his people. And it will be fully realized when the New Jerusalem descends from God out of heaven, and when his tabernacle is with men, and he dwells with them as his people [Rev. 21:3].

What gift is greater than that of God himself? What more can he give than himself—himself with all his virtues and perfections, with his grace and wisdom, with his righteousness and omnipotence, with his immutability and faithfulness? For if God is for us, then who will be against us [Rom. 8:31]? Whatever we encounter, he is and remains ours, in distress and death, in living and dying, for time and eternity. Indeed, he is not the God of the dead but of the living [Mark 12:27; Luke 20:38]. Blessed are the people whose God is the Lord [Ps. 33:12]!

Furthermore, this promise is still richer because God binds himself to it, not only to be our God but also the God of our seed [Gen. 17:7]. If God had given his communion to a few people who stood in no connection to one another, if God proceeded arbitrarily and without taking into account generation, detaching his chosen from all historical connection with flesh and blood, the promise would be great. But the Lord does not act like that. He establishes his covenant organically with man, in Christ as head, first with Adam and then with Abraham, who is a father of all believers.[2] God follows the generational line with grace. He joins creation and re-creation. He executes election through the covenant. He walks, as the Father of all mercy, in the path that he himself has, as Father of all things, assigned. Therefore, the covenant of grace is also eternal in this sense: that in history it continues from generation to generation and is never torn down. Grace is a stream that after the Fall begins to dig itself a bed in human history and ultimately flows into eternity. As a covenant, it may pass through different administrations and appear in distinctive forms; but nevertheless through the omnipotence of God, it has become an ineradicable part of the world and an indestructible good for mankind.

Just because it is a covenant, it carries this incorruptible character. In all covenants there are two parts. First, it is God who gives himself to us; but then from that, we are also warned by God and committed to a new obedience. That is, we cleave to this one God—Father, Son, and Holy Spirit—we trust in him and love him with all our hearts, with all our souls, with all our minds, and with all our strength; we forsake the world, put to death our old nature, and walk in a godly life [Deut. 6:5; Matt. 22:37]. When God gives himself to us, then he wills that subsequently we also will give ourselves entirely, undivided, unconditionally to him with our souls and our bodies, with our strength and talents, with our money and possessions, with our children and grandchildren.[3] Above all, we give our children, who are an inheritance from the Lord and his most valuable earthly blessing. They must be God's, because we are God's.

Nevertheless, when God in the covenant also demands our children for his services, he remains preeminent; he who glorifies the richness of his grace through us and our children [Eph. 2:7]. He is preeminent, when he calls Adam and Noah, Abraham and Israel into his communion, but he also remains this when he admits their children into his covenant. "I will . . . be God to you and to your offspring after you" [Gen. 17:7]. So this is the promise with which God binds himself to the elect in their generations. And before our children were born, or they had done either good or evil, it is he who said in his free, almighty power: "I will be gracious to whom I will be gracious, and will show mercy on whom I will show mercy" [Exod. 33:19].

Our children do not come into that covenant because we dedicate them to the Lord. Much less do they enter because they themselves are worthy of inclusion through some virtue or merit. But they are in by virtue of the promises of God; they are born into it and are in it from the beginning of their existence—not by nature but by grace, because God himself has covenanted to be the God of believers and of their seed.

In the spiritual, the same law prevails as in the natural. We are all participants of a natural life, which we have received through our parents from God, the Almighty, Creator of heaven and earth. That we possess this life is not self-evident. We have not given it to ourselves, we have not merited it, and we have by our own fault even forfeited it. It is in an absolute sense a gift, to be sure, not of God's special but of God's common grace.[4] We become participants of it through conception and birth, in which we are entirely passive. Without any volition of consciousness or will, we are placed in a world that is filled with rich blessings and we enter into the mighty inheritance of our ancestors. We stand upon their shoulders and enjoy what they acquired and brought together by the sweat of their brow.[5]

All of this still applies even more strongly to the spiritual blessings of the covenant. After all, it is not true that for a while we first wander about outside of the covenant and then by faith and conversion come into that covenant, as if by an act of our own will. For faith and conversion are not conditions outside of the covenant of grace, but they are profits and benefits in that covenant, assuming union with Christ and opening the door to the enjoyment of his benefits.

All these benefits—namely, of forgiveness and renewal, holiness and blessedness—come to us only through the Mediator, who secured them with the price of his blood. They cannot be our portion, unless we have a portion in the person of Christ. The mystical union with Christ precedes all benefits and reveals itself first in faith and conversion. As our natural life is given to us in birth and subsequently reveals itself in acts of the intellect and will, even so the spiritual life becomes our possession through regeneration, thereafter bearing fruits of faith and conversion.

And again, it is impossible to have communion with Christ unless the Father gives us Christ as a gift [John 6:44]. The offering and the gift of Christ precedes all his benefits. It is God who in Christ gives us himself and in communion with him gradually gives us all the benefits of the covenant, making us participants in the whole of salvation.

Baptism is the sign and seal of this unspeakable gift of God's grace. For anyone who is baptized in truth is surely washed from the uncleanness of the soul. That is, he is washed from all his sins with the blood of Christ and his Spirit, in the same way water is used to wash away the external uncleanness of the body.

Baptism is, after all, a baptism in the name of the Triune God. At the moment when we are baptized in the name of the Father, God the Father seals us and establishes an eternal covenant of grace with us, adopting us as his children and heirs. Therefore, he will provide us with every good thing, defend us from all evil, or turn that evil to our best. And when we are baptized in the name of the Son, the Son seals us. He washes us in his blood from all our sins, bringing us into communion with his death and resurrection, so that we are saved from all our sins and counted as righteous before God [2 Cor. 1:21–22]. Likewise, when we are baptized in the name of the Holy Spirit, the Holy Spirit by this Holy Sacrament guarantees that he will dwell in us and sanctify us as members of Christ, applying to us that which we have in Christ—namely, the washing away of our sins and the daily renewing of our lives—until we are finally presented spotless and without wrinkle among the assembly of the elect in eternity [Eph. 5:27].

Baptism serves as a witness that God will be our God into eternity, being a merciful Father to us, for he has commanded us to baptize all of those who are his in the name of the Father and of the Son and of the Holy Spirit [Matt. 28:19].

In baptism, God provides visible evidence that he gives himself as a gift to us in Christ and that he has adopted us as his children [John 1:12]. This adoption is the foundation of our confession.

2

The Bringing up of a Child for Confession[1]

"Man shall not live by bread alone, but by every word that comes from the mouth of God." (Matt. 4:4)

Through the covenant, God raises up his children to freedom and independence. While election includes only those who will infallibly inherit eternal salvation, the covenant describes the way in which the elect are led to their destination. Election and covenant are therefore not distinguished as a narrower and a broader circle, for they both encompass the same people. However, while in election they are included by themselves, the covenant always considers them in connection with the whole human race.[2]

Therefore, although the covenant maintains the sovereignty of God in the work of redemption in an exceptionally beautiful way, not permitting man to add anything to it, at the same time it does complete justice to man's rational and moral nature—that is, his creation in the image of God. When God receives the glory due his name, man also receives the position and honor that belong to him according to the will of God. God chooses his own so that they will be in Christ, holy and blameless before him in love.

Therefore, Christ appears in the covenant of grace as head of the church. However, he does not eliminate the Christian nor does he force them from their place. He represents them from the beginning to the end, but in such a way that they themselves, also being taught and trained by the Spirit, consciously and willingly live and walk in the covenant. True, the covenant of grace is established with Christ, but through him and by him it expands from there to all those who are his; and it adopts them wholly and entirely, with body and soul, with mind and will and all strength.

Because God works in them both to will and to do his good pleasure, he exhorts and urges them to work out their salvation with fear and trembling [Phil. 2:13; 4:13]. By the grace of God, they are what they are. They can do all things through Christ, who gives them strength [1 Cor. 15:10; Phil. 4:13]. Because Christ lives in them, they themselves live by the faith of the Son of God [Gal. 2:20].

That is why—although children of believers, even before they possess consciousness and will, are already members of the covenant of grace—the work of the parents is emphasized. This work is to teach their children the faith and to cause them to be instructed in the faith, so that they will be nurtured in the fear and admonition of the Lord. All covenants consist of two parts, and the covenant of grace is no exception. It exhorts us to and it requires of us a new obedience. When God says to us "I am God Almighty," he immediately adds, "Walk before me, and be blameless" [Gen. 17:1]. Giving himself to us, he demands that we give all of ourselves to him.

Children, however, are not able immediately to confess for themselves and to walk in that confession. The parents are responsible for them. They are the ones who bear witness at the baptism of their children, and they guarantee their children's Christian education. On the foundation of the adoption to God's side, parents must bring their children to a conscious and voluntary confession of faith.

Here also, the natural is an image of the spiritual. The natural life, which becomes our portion from our parents through conception and birth, is a gift in an absolute sense; it is unmerited and even forfeited in advance. But that life, from the very first moments of its existence, has all sorts of cares and needs protection. It must be cherished and fostered, shielded and guarded, nourished and refreshed. Without nourishment, in the widest sense of the word, it would waste away and perish.

The first and highest cause of this preservation is God. He is not only the Creator but also the Preserver of all things [Col. 1:16–17].

If he did not sustain life, which he called into existence, with his omnipotent and omnipresent power moment by moment, it would immediately sink back into nothingness. God would be able, if this pleased him, to bring about this preservation without any means, even as he preserved Moses for forty days on the mountain and Jesus in the wilderness [Exod. 24:18; 34:28; Matt. 4:1–11; Mark 1:12–13; Luke 4:1–13]. He would be able to bring it about in an unusual way, even as he sent ravens to provide for Elijah at the brook Cherith and nourished Israel for forty years with manna from heaven [Exod. 16:4; 1 Kings 17:2–6].

But as a rule, God's work of preservation is indirect. He uses food and drink to nourish us, and he uses parents, as the natural caregivers, to provide for the many needs of the child. The parents must lay up treasures for the children, and the children live on those treasures. They have not earned them, nor in the least are they entitled to them; the children are purely dependent and live by grace.

Nevertheless, it is not really bread that feeds us, but the word that comes from the mouth of God [Matt. 4:4]. Man cannot live simply by bread alone, but by the word, the command, the power, the blessing that God has placed on the bread and communicated to us. That which nourishes us is what pleases God to provide with power.

What nutrition is to the natural realm, upbringing is to the spiritual realm. It would not be too amazing for God also to preserve a person's whole spiritual life without any means. Nevertheless, it pleases him to allow people to bring up other people and above all with the word to permit them to work toward the forming and growing of the soul. From childhood, it is through the influence of others that mind and heart, conscience and will, disposition and imagination are formed in people. Likewise, in the nourishment of the spiritual life, which comes through regeneration, God does not work in a different way.

Parents are principally instruments in the hand of God, employed to guide the spiritual lives of their children toward maturity. Nature itself already points to this, for it is in the circle of the family that the children receive their life and spend their first years. God in his revelation is compatible with his teaching in nature. Under Israel, the Lord sharpened the duty of the parents: that they should recount the great works that God had done in their midst to their children and their children's children; that they must give an explanation of the ceremonies that take place in their worship, especially those of the Passover; and that they must instruct them in the laws, in the statutes and judgments that God had given to his people. Even as the Lord himself was the Father and Tutor of his people, so the parents must be the physical and spiritual caregivers of their children.

This duty is bound even stronger to the hearts of the parents in the days of the New Testament. Jesus particularly invites the children to himself. He blesses them and promises them the kingdom of heaven [Matt. 19:13–15]. Not less than the parents, the children share in the blessing of Christ. Therefore, the apostles esteem them highly, including them—as well as adults in the community of Christ—and exhorting them to be obedient to their parents *in the Lord*. On parents, they lay the duty not to provoke their children to anger but to nurture them in the instruction and admonition of the Lord [Eph. 6:1–4]. When Christianity entered the world, it restored and sanctified the broken bonds of family life. It gave the husband to the wife, the mother to the children, the children once more to the parents. And under the impression of that moral transformation a church father wrote this beautiful word: "The mother is the glory of the children, the wife the glory of the husband and both are the glory of the wife."[3]

In the present day, schools assist parents in the weighty task of bringing up children. Because the demands of life, both in knowledge and ability, have become so much higher and more extensive, parents themselves are no longer able personally to fulfill the whole task that rests upon them in the bringing up of their children. They no longer have the time or the ability for it. Therefore, the school has come to stand next to the family, which, to be sure, does not relieve parents of their duty but nevertheless comes to offer help in the fulfillment of it. The parents remain called to nurture their children in the instruction and admonition of the Lord. They must see to it that the education given in the school is in conformity with this. But the school continues the education in this direction, bringing Christian education into connection with the requirements that society establishes for its future working members, setting for its goal to form children into godly people, thoroughly equipped for all good works [2 Tim. 3:17].

The church also has a task to fulfill in the education of the children of the covenant. But her work is substantially different from that of family and school. It was above all the Reformation—and among the Reformers, mainly Calvin—who, in the past, once again laid stress on the ecclesiastical instruction of the youth. The catechetical instruction—which the church officially, in the name of the Lord, gives to her youthful, minor members—has this peculiar and incomparable purpose: that it leads the baptized children to take part in full boldness of faith in the Holy Supper and there, in personal independence and freedom, proclaim with the whole church the death of the Lord. The instruction of the church does not include the task that awaits the children in civil and societal life, but it maintains the connection that God has laid between the two signs and seals of his covenant. It seeks to bring covenant children up to maturity, making them conscious confessing members of the church of Christ.

If it happens like this, according to the rule of the word of the Lord, then family, church, and school work together in a beautiful way. They do not stand independent, side by side, and much less in opposition to each other. One does not break down what the other builds up, but together they labor in the one great task: the reformation of humanity to the image and likeness of God. It is one faith and one baptism that tie them together. It is one confession upon which they all rest. It is one view of the world and life that they pass on to their children for comfort and support in the struggle of this earthly life. Each in its own way, and yet in a mutual relation, they warn and teach every person in all wisdom, that they may present that person perfect in Christ Jesus.

3

The Rule of Confession

Your word is a lamp for my feet and a light to my path. (Ps. 119:105)

Family, church, and school must each handle the word of God, which is found in the Holy Scriptures, to bring up a child to confess the name of the Lord. That word is the foundation, the principle, the rule, and, again, therefore the aim of all confession. We would have nothing to confess if God did not give us, in the Scriptures, his truth to confess. The word of God feeds the spiritual life so that, growing in the grace and knowledge of our Lord Jesus Christ, we may, in an independent way, in our own language speak and confess that word before all men.

To be sure, it is neither parents, nor teachers, nor the minister of the word, it is not even the words in themselves that give and preserve life. For here also the testimony of Jesus is applicable: a person cannot live by bread alone; that is the word with nothing more, but by all the strength and blessing that comes from the mouth of God and is attached to that word [Matt. 4:4]. It is neither Paul who plants nor Apollos who waters but God only who gives the growth [1 Cor. 3:6].

Nevertheless, the word of Scripture in the hands of parents and teachers, under the blessing of the Lord, serves to nourish the spiritual life. As food is for the physical, so the word of God is for the spiritual life. "How sweet are your words to my taste, sweeter than honey to my mouth!" [Ps. 119:103].

That word of God comes to us from the first moments of our existence. It does not come to us the first time the Bible lies open before us, when we read it and examine it. Neither do we come into contact with it for the first time, when in the public assembly of believers a minister proclaims it and we listen. That word comes to us from our most early childhood. It comes to us, in the rebuke of our father, in the admonition of our mother, in the instruction of our teacher, in the fellowship of our friends, in the testimony of our conscience, in the experiences of life. It guides our steps. It accompanies us from the cradle to the grave. It never leaves us. It is like a benediction pronounced over our heads: in songs sung to us; in speech to us, it is bound to our hearts; in commands or prohibitions, it is held before us. Through that word, we are always led and guided, admonished and comforted, encouraged and ashamed, convinced of sin and pointed to Christ. It is the very atmosphere in which we breathe from our birth; it is the food, the drink, the air, the sunshine, the rain for our spiritual life, and that all combined together at one time.

That word is always the power. Without being able or wanting to determine when it is already exerting its influence on the conscience and heart of man, it always remains in itself the power of God unto salvation [Rom. 1:16]. Never is it an empty sound, a dead letter, a meaningless phrase. It is always "living and active, sharper than any two-edged sword, piercing to the division of soul and of spirit, of joints and of marrow, and discerning the thoughts and intentions of the heart" [Heb. 4:12]. It is always a hammer that smashes the hard heart of the sinner, a sword of the Spirit that strikes a deadly blow to the proud and self-righteous, a testimony of God that shakes the conscience awake, the seed of regeneration, the power unto sanctification. It is always "profitable for teaching, for reproof, for correction, and for training in righteousness, that the man of God may be complete, equipped for every good work" [2 Tim. 3:16–17]. In a word, it is a means of grace, going before and standing high above the sacraments.

Even there, where it does not bestow a blessing, it still exerts its effect. The demons believe and shudder [James 2:19]. For unbelievers, it is a fragrance of death to death [2 Cor. 2:16]. It is a rock of offense over which the godless stumble [Isa. 8:14; Rom. 9:33; 1 Pet. 2:8]. If it does not soften, it hardens. If it does not warm, it burns. A person never remains the same after coming into contact with it. That person becomes better or worse, but one can never hide behind the shield of neutrality. "For as the rain and the snow come down from heaven and do not return there but water the earth, making it bring forth and sprout, giving seed to the sower and bread to the eater, so shall my word be that goes out from my mouth; it shall not return to me empty, but it shall accomplish that which I purpose, and shall succeed in the thing for which I sent it" [Isa. 55:10–11].

It is God's word, and therein lies the cause of this power. God not only gave Holy Scripture by inspiration, but through God's omnipotent and omnipresent power, it is continually preserved. The gospel, which comes to people from the Scriptures in all sorts of forms and in various ways, is always brought forth and animated by God. It is and always remains his word. It is constantly accompanied by the Holy Spirit, who lives in the church and goes out from the church into the world, convicting the world of sin, righteousness, and judgment [John 16:8]. It is a word that continually proceeds out of the mouth of God that comes to us in Christ and is declared to our heart or conscience by the Spirit of Christ.

Therefore, that word can be and indeed is the food and drink of the spiritual life. It is the means, not the source of grace. God is and remains the giver and dispenser of all grace. God has not equipped or charged any person, priest, word, or sacrament with the dispersal of the treasures of grace. Servants can give the sign, but only God grants that which is signified. God has—and this also is grace—in sovereign power and goodness bound himself under oath to grant with the word, which is administered in full accord with the mind of the Spirit to each and every one who believingly accepts Christ, who is the food and drink of our souls, the bread that descended from heaven, the water of life of which anyone who drinks will never be thirsty again [John 4:14; 6:51].

But to be like this, that word must with a childlike faith be believed and accepted in humility. Even as bread, no matter how robust and nourishing, it only sustains our natural life when our mouth eats it and our body takes it in. In that way, as food for our souls, the word of God strengthens us when, by faith, it is accepted and implanted in our hearts.

Therefore, God has ordained and fit them one for the other. He, who created food, also created the mouth to eat the food. He, who gave the word, also brought about that new life through regeneration that can only be nourished and strengthened through the food of the word.

They are both related and are originally in close connection to each other. The word works and strengthens the spiritual life. And the spiritual life, by virtue of its nature, is naturally drawn toward this food, even as an infant longs for its mother's milk, as the hungry are drawn toward bread, and the thirsty longs for water.

Furthermore, they both come from one Spirit. In the natural realm, knowledge is possible only because the reason in us and the thoughts in the creation, together and in their mutual relation, have been made by that word that in the beginning was with God, which was God and by which all things have been made [John 1:2–3]. It is the same light that illumines both the eye and objects. That same light of knowledge shines in the human reason and in the works of God's hand. And then only does one see and know when both of these beams of light, coming from one fountain, meet each other. "For with you is the fountain of life; in your light do we see light!" [Ps. 36:9].

In the same way, the spiritual man and the word of the Spirit also belong together. It is the same Spirit that is the Spirit of Christ, who brought about the word and preserves it, and who caused the spiritual man to be born in us. In the Scriptures, the Spirit pictures Christ before our eyes, and the Spirit causes him to live in our hearts by faith. In the Scriptures, the Spirit draws the image of Christ for us, and believers are transformed more and more into that image. For "we all, with unveiled face, beholding the glory of the Lord, are being transformed into the same image from one degree of glory to another. For this comes from the Lord who is the Spirit" [2 Cor. 3:18].

Therefore, it is a true mark of spiritual life when our heart yearns after and longs for that word. It is completely natural, just as one who is hungry longs for bread, the thirsty for water, and the sick for medicine. Just as naturally, the one who is spiritual with a holy longing reaches for the word of God and for Christ, who is offered in that word. Those who are spiritual never grow beyond that word. Unlike the mystic's dreams, the word is not used as a ladder to ascend to a certain height, and then to spread one's own wings and support oneself. Anyone who tries to do so will soon fall to earth broken. Anyone who refuses food will soon starve. Anyone who does not heed the word of Christ does not love him [1 John 5:3]. Anyone who rejects medicine has no need of a physician.

But the spiritual person, as long as one lives and with all one's soul, feels bound to that word as the means of communion and fellowship with God, because God has bound himself to that word. It is only in the proportion one is planted in that word that one grows and becomes stronger. As ivy to a wall, the spiritual person holds fast to the word. As one leans upon a rod or a staff on a pilgrimage, so one leans on the word. One becomes increasingly attached to it, and increasingly devoted to it. The spiritual person's love for the word becomes stronger, considers it ever increasing in value, and always finds in it a rich treasure for both heart and life. For the one who is spiritual, it becomes increasingly God's word, a word that comes to that person from God, a letter from one's Father sent from heaven, to be a guide to the Father's house. "Your word is a lamp to my feet and a light to my path" [Ps. 119:105]. "Oh how I love your law! It is my meditation all the day" [Ps. 119:97].

Therefore, parents must feed their covenant child, even from early childhood, with this word. If it is done with wisdom, it cannot begin too early. Already, the respectful attitude of the other members of the household during prayer and the reading of God's word cultivates in the child a realization of the sacred, and that weightiness often sticks in the memory until the last years of life. The short prayer, before and after the meal, and at bedtime and when waking up, often become impressed later, becoming indelible marks and still later in life reminding them of their pious years as a youth. Certainly, one does not need to wait until the children can understand concepts to teach them religious words, as though this would turn them into little hypocrites. For one learns concepts through words even as one learns words through concepts; the one helps the others. There is, in general, a striking similarity between the feeling of dependence and humility, which is inherent in a child by nature, and the posture that God loves to see in us and that is most pleasing to him. If we do not become like little children, we will never enter the kingdom of heaven [Matt. 18:3; Mark 10:15].

But then, this bringing of God's word to children must, at the same time, be both instruction and training, simultaneously working on mind and heart and together focusing on both knowledge and actions. One must guard against the extremes found in both formalistic orthodoxy and pietism. Religion is not only knowledge but also life; the person does not only have consciousness but also feeling and will. God's law demands that we love God not only with our whole mind but also with our whole heart, and soul, and all of our strength [Deut. 4:29; Matt. 22:37; Mark 12:30; Luke 10:27]. Therefore, education—careful and conscientious instruction in the doctrines of truth—must take place so that pure ideas, clear concepts, and correct judgments may be instilled in the child, and a basic knowledge of this truth may be formed in their consciousness. The cultivation of emotions and the awakening of affections without true and clear representations is itself dangerous. It does damage to the truth. It opens the door for error and deception, and it is often leads to gross excesses.

Nevertheless, clear ideas and pure concepts are not enough. Indeed, especially in the realm of religion, these provide almost nothing anywhere, without concurrently being an influence on the feelings and the heart. For, a right understanding, basic knowledge is never obtained without the heart. All learning needs attraction, interest, love. That which is unknown is unloved. One learns and only truly knows that which is loved in the depths of the soul.

Therefore, child-rearing does not follow education. The mind does not come first, and only after—sooner or later—is the heart considered. There are not first pure concepts imprinted, in the hope that later they will be accepted with a true faith of the heart and that those concepts will be able to influence life and actions.

Rather, from the beginning, child-rearing and education must go hand in hand. Education itself ought always to carry with it a child-rearing character. God's truth is of such a nature that it cannot be known rightly without a sincere faith of the heart. Whoever impresses the truth upon their consciousness, without having it in the heart, takes only the image of the things but remains a stranger to the things themselves.

Therefore, the influencing of consciousness and will, the training to know and do, the instilling of clear, pure representations, and the awakening of affections and deep impressions of the soul should always go together. We may not separate the words from the matter, nor the matter from the words, for God has united these two. He has covenanted to give that which is signified to everyone who believes the word in truth. The one who knows God in the face of Christ has eternal life. Thus, when we speak of God, of Christ, etc., these names cannot be mere sounds to us, but we must think of the ones who are signified by them. With this, then, the gospel is rich; it is not an abstract system but a world of unseen, eternal treasures, which are signified and sealed, designated and delivered to us.

If, in this way, home and school and catechism cooperate, united by the truth in education and child-rearing, then it can be expected that under the blessing of the Lord the spiritual life will come to grow and develop. It will flourish in faith and repentance, and soon a public profession of faith will be made with both mouth and heart.

It always remains true, however, that this growth must come from above [James 1:17]. "Unless the Lord builds the house, those who build it labor in vain" [Ps. 127:1]. Parents, teachers, and ministers are only instruments in the Lord's hand. He is the only true Father and trainer of his children, who feeds and leads, preserves and protects, strengthens and perfects them. "Nor is he served by human hands, as though he needed anything, since he himself gives to all mankind life and breath and everything" [Acts 17:25; cf. Job 12:10]. He rules by the power of the word and the working of the Spirit. Jesus is the vine, the believers are the branches, and the heavenly Father is the gardener [John 15].

4

The Essence of Confession

If you confess with your mouth that Jesus is Lord and believe in your heart that God raised him from the dead, you will be saved. For with the heart one believes and is justified, and with the mouth one confesses and is saved. (Rom. 10:9–10)

Everything that lives and grows has need of time. While a machine can be put together quickly in just a few moments, life and growth cannot be forced. Artificial acceleration of growth produces greenhouse plants that cannot withstand either tempest or thunderstorm.

The spiritual life is also subject to the law of development of organic beings. Holy Scripture knows all sorts of differences among the children of God [Rev. 7:9]. It speaks of lambs and sucklings among the sheep in Jesus' flock. It mentions children, youths, and fathers in the faith. It distinguishes between minors and adults and between milk and a steady diet of the truth, which must be administered to believers [Isa. 40:11; Matt. 18:2; 1 Cor. 3:2; Heb. 5:12]. Time and again, it admonishes the believer to grow in the knowledge and grace of the Lord Jesus Christ, to put on the new man fashioned after God in true righteousness and holiness, to be strengthened in the inner man and renewed in the spirit of the mind [2 Pet. 3:18; Eph. 4:23–24].

Just as the natural life must be developed, so also the spiritual life. It must not remain hidden from people, neither can it be buried as a treasure in a field [Matt. 13:44]. It cannot be doomed to inactivity. Life is a stranger to all stagnation. Life is movement, life is strength, life is action. All that lives moves and develops. It can be hampered and opposed in its growth, but as long as there is life, the effect is inseparable from it. To a still much greater extent, this applies to the spiritual life, which is implanted through the Holy Spirit and bears an eternal, indestructible character [Ezek. 36:26–27; Eph. 1:13–14]. Wherever it is, it reveals itself, it goes forth in both word and deed, and it develops into the activities of faith and conversion. If faith is present, confession is thereby freely given [Col. 3:16–17].

Confession is a glorious word for a still more excellent and glorious thing. However, it has in many respects lost its beauty and strength for our minds. When we use it or hear others use it, generally we immediately think of the confessional statements of this or that Christian church. We may also think of the public confession that the young members of the congregation make at some point in their life for admission to the Lord's Supper. Yet, these meanings of the word *confession* are derived. The original sense in Scripture is much richer and deeper. It is nothing different from or less than someone's public witness in word and deed of personal faith in Jesus as the Christ [Rom. 10:9; Matt. 10:32; Phil. 2:11].

Two things are then included in this. First, a true, genuine faith is a deep, firm conviction of the heart. No confession is possible, in any real sense, if faith is not present in the heart [Acts 8:37]. Confession is a thing of the heart. It is rooted in the heart. It comes up out of the heart. It is a fruit of the heart. Without that faith, confession becomes useless lip service, an external repetition with the mouth, an impersonal, untrue, hypocritical act that is not worthy of the beautiful name of "confession." Jesus fought against and condemned this type of Pharisaism in his own day with holy wrath [Matt. 23; Titus 1:6]: Hypocrites are like whitewashed tombs [Matt. 23:27].

Second, faith of the heart is not ashamed of itself but gives a public witness. The one who does not believe cannot confess [Rom. 10:8–10]. But the one who does believe in truth and uprightness must confess. That person cannot remain silent. That person must speak in the presence of friend and foe, before the face of God, angels, and men [Acts 4:20]. Whatever slander may be associated, whatever hatred and persecution it arouses—the one who believes speaks loudly, powerfully, and freely. We believe, and therefore we speak [Ps. 116:10; 2 Cor. 4:13].

Jeremiah made himself a mockery among his people because of his prophesying. Nevertheless, he could not be silent. The Lord overwhelmed him. The Lord was too strong for him and triumphed over him. Even if he said, "I will not mention him, or speak any more in his name," the word the Lord placed in his heart became like a burning fire shut up in his bones [Jer. 20:9]. When the lion roars, who will not fear? When the Lord speaks, who will not prophesy [Amos 3:8]?

Therefore, believing with the heart and confessing with the mouth go together and belong to each other inseparably [Rom. 10:8–10]. Whoever believes and does not confess is in just as much conflict with the Lord's will as the one who confesses and does not believe. As a certain church father said, both are necessary—a true, firm faith and a free confession—so that the heart is adorned with the certainty of faith and the tongue may boldly confess the truth. And another testified: The heart needs the mouth, for what fruit does it produce to believe with the heart without publicly confessing before men? The faith of the heart may justify, nevertheless, and confession lifts up this perfect salvation. Faith first shines when it declares itself in confession, and through this many are benefitted. On the other hand, the mouth needs the heart, for there are many who confess Christ but whose hearts are far from him [Matt. 15:8].

The apostle Paul also speaks this way when he says that the faith of the heart gives righteousness but that the confession of the mouth must accompany it to obtain salvation [Rom. 10:9]. To be sure, it is true that these two cannot be separated, no more than the confession of the Lord Jesus can be separated from faith in his resurrection. Faith without confession cannot give righteousness, and confession without faith cannot give salvation. Faith and confession are as inextricably bound together as the lordship of Jesus and his resurrection from the dead, and as inseparably as righteousness and salvation [1 Cor. 15:12–19]. Yet, it is true—and this is what the apostle Paul wants to point out—that, although the faith of the heart justifies, it first manifests itself as the true, justifying faith when it proclaims itself in confession. Faith, not confession, justifies. But that this faith is the true faith, the faith that leads to salvation, first becomes evident in the confession. True, justifying faith leads to salvation only by way of confession. Without holiness, no one will see God. Without confession, as a fruit of faith, no one will enter heaven. Confession is not the cause for meriting salvation, but it is the royal way to salvation.

Faith and confession therefore also exert an influence on each other and are mutually encouraging and supportive. The faith that does not make confession becomes shy, timid, retreats, languishes, or even finds itself to be inauthentic and unreliable. Confession without faith is a flower without a stem; it withers and falls to pieces. On the other hand, through confession, faith gains strength. It is planted, and its roots shoot still deeper into the soil of the heart. Through faith, confession receives its fervor and inspiration. It gains courage and boldness. It is as though through some unseen power it is constantly preserved and fed.

From this it then also follows that the so-called public confession of faith is not a detached, self-contained act that takes place once and then is done forever. That kind of education still occurs many times. A few weeks beforehand, they prepare themselves for the solemn hour of confession. They abstain from public entertainment, going more regularly to church and catechism. On the day of confession, they put on new clothing. Perhaps afterward, they partake in the Lord's Supper. But then everything is forgotten. Life continues as if nothing had happened.

Such a confession is wholly unworthy of the name "confession." It is no more than a work, accepted and delivered. Such a confession has become an old habit, which is kept up thoughtlessly and without any will.

That is not confessing the faith. Confession has a much richer sense and a much deeper meaning. Certainly, it is a serious act and a solemn hour when young members give their confession of personal faith for the first time in the midst of the congregation. It is a landmark along the way of life, an entry into all the rights Christ grants to his believers. We proclaim this "yes," and we are bound to it for time and eternity. God holds us to it and will judge us according to it. Christ continues to remember it and will call for an account of it. The Holy Spirit will keep it in our memory and will point us to it until our dying day, even into eternity. If it does not testify for us, it will in the last day testify against us. It will fly in our face and make our condemnation all the heavier.

A confession of faith is not something that stands by itself with no connection to that which precedes and follows it. It is not a sacrament as Rome has made it. It bears in itself no special supernatural holiness. It is not separated, as by a fence, from the realm of common life. It does not incorporate us into a new company of soldiers under Christ Jesus as king. However important and serious the making of public confession of faith is, it does not stand detached by itself but is closely connected with that which precedes and follows confession.

Daily confession precedes this one-time public confession. All faith confesses according to its own degree, in its own way and language—be it the faith of the playing child, the happy boy, or the lively youth. If faith is the true mark, if only true, childlike fear of God is in the heart, then this always occurs. It reveals itself in the piousness of desires, the uprightness of mind, the tenderness of heart, the respect for the holy, the yearning to pray, the fear of evil, and in restraining one's self and others from what is wrong and sinful. Confession is what our children already do from childhood, and their confession is lovely to the ears of God. What does Scripture say? Let the little children come to me and hinder them not, for theirs is the kingdom of heaven [Matt. 19:14]. Because the name of the Lord is majestic over all the earth, out of the mouth of babes and infants he establishes the strength to leave the enemy silent [Ps. 8:2]. God chooses the small and weak to shame the great and mighty [1 Cor. 1:27]. Children in their simplicity, uprightness, and humility are preachers of the glory of the Lord that extends over all the earth and is most richly revealed in Christ. Just as the childhood confession of faith precedes the public confession, so also that public confession is followed by confession throughout the whole of life, even until the hour of death.

It is true that the primary purpose of public confession of faith in the midst of the congregation is to serve to admit someone to the Lord's Supper. It opens the access to the table of the covenant. Therefore, confession seems to separate baptism and the Lord's Supper from each other. But, indeed, this is not the case. Rather, confession binds the two and holds them together.

It should be this way. Baptism and the Lord's Supper are sacraments of identical value. They have the same power and significance. They are signs and seals of the same covenant. The word directs and rules both of them, so that they point our faith to the sacrifice of Jesus Christ on the cross as the only ground of our salvation. These two sacraments are also given to the same believers. In the New Testament, baptism was mostly administered to adults. Confession, therefore, preceded baptism. Whoever was baptized had immediate admission to the Lord's Table.

However, when infant baptism became generally acceptable, a gradual separation came about. Nevertheless, baptism can be administered to children of the covenant, for it is the sacrament of regeneration and incorporation into the church of Christ. Yet, the Lord's Supper presupposes that we ourselves accept the broken bread and eat, that we ourselves receive the cup and drink. Therefore, the right administration of the Lord's Supper must be preceded by the ability to examine ourselves and discern the body of the Lord. It is the sacrament of the growth of the spiritual life in the fellowship of Christ and, therefore, is to be regularly repeated.

Consequently, confession gradually took its place between baptism and the Lord's Supper, not to separate them but on the contrary to hold them together and to lead from baptism to the Lord's Supper. Confession presupposes baptism and prepares for the Lord's Supper. In confession, the baptized person accepts one's own baptism and desires to receive admission to the second sign of the covenant. By the grace of God, this person is adopted as a child of God. And now, having come to the age of discretion and to consciousness of his life, he speaks the confession, humbly and childlike but also piously and surely before all people that God is his God. He puts his hand in the hand of the Lord. He accepts freely and with clear understanding the covenant into which he was incorporated from birth. On account of the Lord's pledge of "I am your God," the Christian now answers, "I am your servant, the son of your maidservant. You have loosed my bonds" [Ps. 116:16]. God raises his children to freedom and independence. He wants a willing people on the day of his power [Ps. 110:3]. We love him because he first loved us [1 John 4:19].

That is what the believer proclaims, when admitted to the Lord's Supper in the solemn hour of his confession. He also makes confession of it, when he later sits with the congregation at the table of the Lord. In the sacrament, the emphasis is certainly placed on what God does—on his gift and on his grace. In it, he offers Christ to us with all the benefits he has acquired. Our Savior Jesus Christ instituted the Lord's Supper specifically to nourish and preserve those whom he had already regenerated and incorporated into his household, which is his church. It is his flesh we eat and his blood we drink with the mouth of faith, for the strengthening of our spiritual life.

But then, in the second place, from the human perspective, the sacrament is a confession of faith. Self-examination precedes the Lord's Supper, which consists in three things. First, we must consider our own sin and cursing, so that we may abhor it and humble ourselves before God. Second, we must examine our own hearts as to whether we believe this trustworthy promise of God—that all our sins, because of the suffering and death of Jesus Christ, are forgiven, and that the perfect righteousness of Christ is imputed and freely given to us as our own. Third, we must examine our own conscience as to whether we are ready from now on to show true thankfulness to God in our whole life and to walk uprightly before him.

What a significant confession we make, therefore, when we go to the Lord's Supper! We do not come to it to testify that we are perfect and righteous in ourselves; but on the contrary, because we seek our life outside of ourselves—namely, in Jesus Christ—we acknowledge that we lie in the midst of death. In this sacrament, we confess that Jesus Christ is the true food and drink of our souls, and we are members of his body. As it is one bread, so we being many are one body, for we all share in the one bread [1 Cor. 10:17].

However, the Lord's Supper does not stand far outside and highly above our life. Certainly, it is extraordinary in this sense—that God always comes to us anew in it with great grace, placing it before our eyes, and securing it to our hearts. Very often, the Lord's Supper seems strange and wonderful to us because it is celebrated only a few times in a year and then not faithfully by all. But the grace that is given to us in the sacrament is none other than that which constantly accompanies the word of the gospel and feeds us day by day. Therefore, in the beginning, Christian congregations celebrated the Lord's Supper not only every Sabbath but also at the weekly meetings of the believers. It was the high point of the worship service, the communion of saints, the sustenance they constantly receive for their pilgrimage.

The Lord's Supper signs and seals the communion with Christ. We possess this communion at all times in the word and enjoy it through faith. We give evidence of that faith, not only when we sit at the table of the covenant, but also on Sunday when we go up to the house of prayer with the congregation.

As surely as we are sincere believers, we confess this faith throughout our whole life, for faith cannot do otherwise: it must confess. It does not ask whether good works must be done; but before the question can even arise, it has already done them. Confession with mouth and heart, word and deed, in conduct and behavior is inseparable from the faith of the heart. It is the fruit of the tree, the scent of the flower, the light of the sun, the sweetness of the honey. It is impossible that anyone grafted into Christ by a true faith should not bring forth fruits of thankfulness.[1] Whoever believes confesses, not only on Sunday but also during the week, not only in the church but also at home and school, in the shop and factory, in the office and store, in civil and societal life, in science and art, among friends and enemies, before angels and people.

This person confesses in the supporting of the public worship of the church, in the act of Christian aid, in the promoting of education, in the care for the poor, in the visitation of the prisoner, in the clothing of the naked, in the feeding of the hungry, in the comforting of the mourning, in the admonition of the unruly, in refutation of opponents, in the giving of an account of the hope that lies within, in keeping oneself unspotted from the world. Whoever believes, confesses, and that person's life itself becomes a confession—a living, holy offering in Christ that is pleasing to God.

5

The Contents of Confession

And Philip said, "If you believe with all your heart, you may." And he replied, "I believe that Jesus Christ is the Son of God." (Acts 8:37)

In particular two items constitute the contents of confession according to Holy Scripture.

In the first place, all true confession contains an acknowledgment of our guilt and sin. In the days of the Old Testament, on the Day of Atonement, the high priest was required to lay both of his hands upon the head of a live goat, confessing all the iniquities and transgressions of the children of Israel, regardless of the nature of their sins. When with this symbolic act, he had laid the sins of the people upon the head of the goat, he needed to send the goat away into the wilderness [Lev. 16:20–22].

That was a communal confession made by the high priest on behalf of the whole nation. But this communal confession did not exclude the personal, individual confession of sins. This is constantly mentioned in the books of the old covenant, especially in the so-called penitential psalms.[1] It also forms a prominent element of the prayers of the saints, of David and Solomon, of Isaiah and Jeremiah and Daniel. There exists not a people in the world that have felt so deeply the guilt of sin and have confessed so humbly as the children of Israel.

> My iniquities have overtaken me, and I cannot see; they are more than the hairs of my head. [Ps. 40:12]

> There is no health in my bones because of my sin. For my iniquities have gone over my head; like a heavy burden, they are too heavy for me. [Ps. 38:3–4]

> Enter not into judgment with your servant, for no one living is righteous before you. [Ps. 143:2]

> If you, O Lord, should mark iniquities, O Lord, who could stand? [Ps. 130:3]

This confession of sins continues in the church of the New Testament. When John the Baptist appeared and preached repentance, many were baptized by him in the Jordan and confessed their sins [Luke 3:1–21]. Jesus often not only healed the multitude of sick who came to him with their bodily diseases, but he also gave an even greater gift—namely, the forgiveness of their sins and the salvation of their soul [Col. 1:14]. He placed this prayer on the lips of his disciples: Father, "forgive us our debts, as we also have forgiven our debtors" [Matt. 6:12]. In the parable of the tax collector, he portrays the spirit in which we as sinners come before the righteous and holy God. The tax collector standing far off would not even lift up his eyes to heaven but beat his chest, saying, "God, be merciful to me, a sinner!" [Luke 18:13]. If we confess our sins, God is true and faithful and righteous and will forgive us our sins and cleanse us from all unrighteousness [1 John 1:9].

But no matter how necessary this confession of sins is, alone it is insufficient. The doctrine of our misery does not stand by itself but prepares the way for redemption and gratitude. Indeed, whoever sees and confesses his sins and misery is already a believer [Prov. 28:13]. On the Lord's Days of the Heidelberg Catechism that treat the misery of man, it is not the unbeliever but the Christian who speaks, one who already in the first division has gloried in his only comfort and confessed that he with body and soul, both in life and death, is no longer his own but belongs to his faithful Savior Jesus Christ.[2]

The true, genuine confession of guilt is already a fruit of saving faith. For whoever in truth and humility confesses his sins has certainly already sought the Lord; he has placed himself before God's countenance and finds himself in the presence of the Almighty. This cannot be done apart from the belief that the Lord is gracious and abounding in steadfast love [Exod. 34:6; Ps. 103:8].

To be sure, there is a certain acknowledgement of sins that occurs outside of faith. Children of the world also sometimes come to recognize the great miserableness of their existence. Cain said, "My punishment is greater than I can bear," and Judas cried out, "I have sinned by betraying innocent blood" [Gen. 4:13; Matt. 27:4]. There is a cry of despair that is not borne out of a broken heart but that is brought forth by the terrible consequences of sin. There is a remorse and despondency that does not drive one toward God but that causes one to flee from and rebel against God. There is a sorrow of the world that produces not a repentance that leads unto salvation but that works death [2 Cor. 7:10].

However, the true confession of sins is different from this cry of despair and bears another character completely. It comes up out of a contrite spirit, which is not despised by God but pleasing to him. It is contrite not about the consequences but the essence, the guilt of sin, because it displeases God and is contrary to his law. It consists in heartfelt grief: that by our sin we have provoked God to anger; that against his righteousness and even more grievously against his love, we have sinned. As Jesus once said, "If I had not come and spoken to them, they would not have been guilty of sin, but now they have no excuse for their sin" [John 15:22].

This confession is accompanied with a sorrow toward God and produces a repentance that leads to salvation without regret [2 Cor. 7:10]. It is made before God's face and holds nothing back from him. It is accompanied by and is born of a faith that God is not only righteous but also gracious and merciful. It is also already a confession of faith; it is from and through and to faith [Rom. 11:36]. Faith does not first begin after the knowledge of misery but precedes it and provides it with the right form. Above the law are the words of grace: "I am the Lord your God" [Exod. 20:2]. True conversion is a fundamental component of gratitude.

That is why Scripture says, in the second place, that confession includes a confession of the name of the Lord [Rom. 10:9;

1 Cor. 12:3]. Repentance and confession of the Lord's name belong together. For the confession of God's name signifies the heartfelt, believing acknowledgment that the Lord is the God of the covenant, who has revealed himself as gracious and faithful, fulfilling all of his promises of grace in Christ [2 Cor. 1:20]. Whoever repents with a true heart has turned to God, the living God, who is a reconciled Father in Christ [2 Cor. 5:18].

Just as in the days of the New Testament when John the Baptist appeared, he proclaimed not only repentance and confession of sins but also pointed to the Lamb of God "who takes away the sin of the world!" [John 1:29]. He was not a preacher of the law and of repentance only but also a herald of the gospel and a preacher of faith. "The kingdom of heaven is at hand" [Matt. 3:2]. After him came the one who was before him, "the sandals of whose feet I am not worthy to untie" [Acts 13:25]. John administered baptism as a sign and seal of the forgiveness of sins, which is granted and obtained on the road of repentance.

At every turn in the New Testament, the entire content of the confession of faith goes hand in hand with the little phrase that Jesus is "the Christ, the Son of the living God" [Matt. 16:16]. Whoever confesses him as such before others, Christ will also one day confess him before his Father who is in heaven [Matt. 10:32]. In a sincere moment when many of Jesus' disciples went back and no longer desired to walk with him, he asked the Twelve: "Do you want to go away as well?" But Simon Peter answered for them all: Lord, to whom shall we go? You have the words of eternal life, and we have believed, and have come to know, that you are the Holy One of God Christ, the Son of the living God" [Matt 16:16; John 6:66–69].[3] Likewise, as soon as the eunuch made this good confession, he was immediately baptized by Philip [Acts 8:26–40]. It is by the confession that Jesus Christ has come in the flesh that the spirits are known [1 John 4:2]. Therefore, "whoever confesses that Jesus is the Son of God, God abides in him, and he in God" [1 John 4:15].

Jesus is the promised Messiah, the divinely anointed prophet, priest, and king—that is the brief contents of the whole Christian faith. It is the heart of revelation, the heart of Holy Scripture, the bone and marrow of all confession, the central dogma of all the truths of salvation, the center from which all the rays of knowledge of God expand to the periphery. The person of Christ determines the essence of Christianity.

With this confession, the church of Christ took its own independent place in the midst of Jews and Gentiles. By it, she was distinguished from them both. For from her confession, she came to an ever-richer development of her faith and life. At first, everyone was baptized who made confession of the Lord Jesus. Before long, this confession was enhanced to that of the name of the Father, the Son, and the Holy Spirit. In the twelve articles of our indubitably catholic Christian faith, this baptismal confession receives an even greater development.[4] Finally, in the various confessions of the Christian church, all of these articles have been more closely studied and further explained. The confessions are like branches and leaves proceeding from a single root—that in the beginning, planted in the soil of the church, was the belief that Jesus is the Christ.

To be sure, creation and the Fall, sin and misery are assumed in this short confession of faith. The whole person of Christ, with his names and natures, with his offices and states, lies as if it were in seed form. The whole order of salvation—for the individual, for humanity, for the world—is intricately included in it. In the cross of Christ, which is an offense to the Jews and foolishness to the Greeks, sin and grace, law and gospel, justice and mercy, guilt and forgiveness are united and reconciled [1 Cor. 1:23]. God and the world, heaven and earth, angels and humanity, peoples and nations extend to one another the hand of peace by that cross. For by the cross of Christ, God has reconciled the world to himself—not imputing her trespasses against her—and God has triumphed over all authority and powers [2 Cor. 5:19]. In the grace of our Lord Jesus Christ, we participate in the love of the Father and enjoy the fellowship of the Holy Spirit [2 Cor. 13:14].

6

The Diversity of Confession

"We hear them telling in our own tongues the mighty works of God." (Acts 2:11)

In the early days of the church, this short confession—that Jesus is the Christ, the Son of the living God—was sufficient. But this time of simple, childlike faith did not last long and could not endure. Conflicts from without, as well as thoughts that arose from within, urged the church to give a clearer account of the substance of its faith.

And from that moment, all kinds of disagreements and conflicts revealed themselves. Before long, the unity of confession was gone for good. Although through all kinds of coercive measures the church and state always tried to preserve unity, even if only by appearance, yet the process of splitting and division has continued even to the present day. Disagreement and discord are ubiquitous among Christians. Churches and individuals in the name of Christ and with an appeal to his word find themselves standing in hostile opposition to one another. Yet the multiformity of the Christian faith continually increases. One can hardly imagine a restoration of unity.

This division of Christianity is a great disappointment. For we have indeed only one God, "the Father, from whom are all things and for whom we exist, and one Lord, Jesus Christ, through whom are all things and through whom we exist" [1 Cor. 8:6]. The church "is one body and one Spirit—just as you were called to the one hope that belongs to your call—one Lord, one faith, one baptism" [Eph. 4:4–5]. Jesus himself prayed for the unity of his disciples, that the world might believe that the Father had sent him [John 17]. Thus we might also expect that the confession that flows from the lips of the church should be one.

What is more, the existing division is not only a grievous disappointment, but it is also a great sin before God. As Christians, we cannot humble ourselves enough on account of it. It is a weighty indictment against us, because it principally has its cause in the darkness of our understandings and the uncharitableness of our hearts.

Nor may this division be glossed over by saying that the confessions, which have gradually come to stand side by side in the Christian church, should be regarded as different expressions of one and the same truth. For these confessions do not differ only in language and style, words and expressions, but the articles of faith themselves often stand in contradiction to each other, so that one affirms what another denies. Election through grace or because of a foreseen faith, justification by faith alone or because of the works of love, the spiritual or corporeal presence of Christ in the Supper are not differences in name only, but they are beliefs that contradict each other. The diversity of confessions must not be confused with the errors that can sneak in because of the darkness of our understanding. We cannot and may not, therefore, be indifferent or neutral with respect to the confessions that have emerged and now continue to exist side by side in the Christian church. We may appreciate the good intentions of those Christians, who in former or latter times, have attempted to preserve or bring about this very much desired unity in the church of Christ, either in a compulsory or artificial way.

Yet, we must take into account the fact that all these attempts, in spite of our best intentions, result only in the truth being falsified and freedom being suppressed, and often disagreement still increases. For whoever withdraws himself from all parties out of objectivity runs the risk of becoming the head of a new party himself.

Furthermore, it must never be forgotten that God's hand is also on history, with all its injustice and errors, and that he executes his wise counsel in history. His providence governs all things so that nothing occurs by chance, least of all in the Christian church over which Christ has in a special sense been appointed head and king by the Father [Col. 1:18; Rev. 19:16]. The ever-increasing divisions in Christendom is a fact that cannot take place outside God's control—it is included and determined in his counsel and with it, therefore, doubtlessly he has his own high and wise purposes.

Even though the sin that is both created and appears in division can in no way be ignored, it is unfair to under-appreciate the various benefits that have been gained through this division and conflict. What man has thought evil, God has often meant for good [Gen. 50:20]. Out of darkness, he can bring forth light; out of death, life; out of the shame of mankind, he brings glory to his name. So far is God from godlessness and the Almighty from injustice that he can both constrain and use sin to labor for the glory of his grace and the establishment of his kingdom.

As soon as the truth, as it was revealed in Christ and proclaimed by the apostles, reflected itself in the human mind, it was almost immediately robbed of its purity and all sorts of errors were mixed in; heresies and schisms already began in the days of the apostles. Yet, the truth also gradually became clearer in its richness and multifaceted meaning. It is through the eye of faith that the church always gets deeper insight into the mysteries of salvation that God has deposited and revealed for it in his word.

To be sure, people are already endlessly different from each other in the natural life. Gender and age, talents and character, education and environment, country and people, time and place, class and position, and diversity of gifts of intellect and heart all bring about the greatest changes in the opinion and view of things. No two people are exactly alike.

And this diversity that exists in nature is not erased by grace. For grace does not suppress and destroy nature but restores and renews it. Still, grace expands the natural diversity through the diversity of spiritual gifts that, to be sure, are all worked by the one and the same Spirit. However, that Spirit dispenses unique gifts to everyone, according to his will.

In unity, God loves diversity. The whole of creation testifies to this: nature with its mountains and valleys, with its seas and islands;

the earth with its kingdoms of minerals and plants, of animals and men; the heavens with its planets and stars; and the heaven of heavens with its thousands of holy angels. The glory of the infinitely rich essence of God is reflected in the works of his hands. God's grace and attributes are revealed in creation.

We see this diversity still clearer and fuller in re-creation—starting with Christ, who is the most beautiful of all the children of men, from whose lips grace and truth poured out. Around Christ in colorful, packed rows are the patriarchs and prophets, the apostles and evangelists, the martyrs and reformers, and the whole host of the redeemed who are bought with his blood and renewed by his Spirit. They are different in heaven from how they were different on earth. That diversity, even through the error and guilt of man, ends up at the knowledge of truth and the glory of God's good grace. Christ takes it into service and adorns his church with it. The Holy Spirit uses it to have everyone in their own language declare the great works of God. One day at the end of time, God will receive all the glory through the church from every language and people, tribe and nation [Rev. 7:9].

For this reason, it is no wonder that in all the diversity of confession the different relationship in which grace places itself to nature is reflected. The essence of the Christian religion consists in this—that the creation of the Father, ruined by sin, is again restored in the death of the Son of God and through the grace of the Holy Spirit is re-created into the kingdom of God. The great question therefore that always and everywhere returns is this: What is the relationship in which grace places itself to nature? Practically every person must settle that relation for himself in his thinking and life, in his willing and acting. In ever expanding spheres, it continually comes up in church and state, in family and society, and in art and science. What is the relation between the creation and re-creation, of the kingdoms of the earth and the kingdom of heaven, of humanity and Christianity, of that which is from below and that which is from above?

Depending on his own personal peculiarity, each person will define this relationship differently and will also apply it differently in his life. It makes a great difference whether we think of grace as a doctrine or as life; whether it is considered as a divine supplement to nature or as a remedy against the sickness of sin; whether it is intended only for the heart and private space, or for the whole richness of human life; whether it only serves to save the soul or has the scope of preparing glory for God from all his works. Because of this difference, among believers, even among members of one and the same church, emerge all sorts of smaller and bigger differences in confession. To be sure, the truth is one, but it reflects itself in the consciousness of man in different ways. Indeed, only one sun shines in the heaven, but everyone sees it with his own eye.

In these and other such differences, in which one or another side of the truth is seen or put to the foreground, the differences in the confession of the Christian church certainly do not fully arise. Nevertheless, even if these differences are so great, we must not overlook the unity that is clearly revealed in them. We are prone to run the risk of being one-sided. It cannot be denied that there is difference and controversy over many articles of faith. However, staring at that which divides believers one from the other, we too easily forget that which unites and holds them together. Often, the harmony is too deeply veiled from our view by the discord that exists.

And yet, there is also consensus. Believers are all one, not exclusively in the spiritual sense, for they all are together grafted into Christ and are members of his body; but also in an external sense, that a visible bond encircles all Christian churches and confessions and separates them from all non-Christians [Rom. 11:17].

To some extent, there is no Christianity beyond the divisions of faith. The differences between innumerable Christian churches and confessions have not been mechanically added to the points of agreement. One cannot deduct the first from the last so that a perfect equal sum remains. Every confession is an organic whole. The Roman is Romish, even in the confession of the twelve articles of faith, which has been adopted by all churches. Reformed and Lutherans, Baptists and Remonstrants are distinguished from each other not only in the doctrine of election, church, and sacraments, but also in those of God, Christ, creation and providence, redemption and justification.

But there is, nevertheless, a Christianity in the divisions of faith—a unity that, rightly viewed, is much greater and infinitely more significant than all that which divides and separates believers from each other. Although that unity must be detached from the diversity, it is nevertheless truly and really present in it, and it also reveals itself clearly and plainly prior to that day. Although written confessions often limit themselves to the exposition of differences, in the unwritten articles, the prayers, the fruits of faith, and the works of mercy a striking harmony comes to light. The flawed confession of the lips very often fails to do justice to the faith of the heart.

Thus it appears to be the counsel and will of the Lord that the unity of faith and knowledge of the Son of God through diversity and even opposition clears the way for the coming of the glorious end of history. When in the future, the body of Christ has attained full maturity and comes to be perfect to the extent of the great fullness of Christ, then all the saints together will fully understand each other and the breadth and length and depth and height of the love of Christ that surpasses all understanding, that they may be filled with all the fullness of God [Eph. 3:18–19].

7

The Universality of Confession

So let no one boast in men. For all things are yours, whether Paul or Apollos or Cephas or the world or life or death or the present or the future—all are yours, and you are Christ's and Christ is God's. (1 Cor. 3:21–23)

The diversity of confession does not violate its universality. Although there are many churches, yet as Christians we altogether confess the same one, holy universal church, which manifests itself in the many and various churches of Christendom, although very often in an imperfect way.

Universal, catholic, is the Christian confession in this sense, that it spreads itself over the whole earth, includes all true believers, applies to all people, and has significance for the whole world. Christianity is a world religion, destined for every status and class, place and time. The church that is most catholic has expressed this international and cosmopolitan character of the Christian religion in the purity of confession and applied it the most widely in practice.

This universality of the Christian religion is directly related to the unity of God, which is taught in it. God is one and therefore his words and works can never contradict each other. All things have their relation and system in his consciousness, in his will, in his counsel. They all exist together in the Son, who is the image of the invisible God, the firstborn of all creation, through whom and to whom all things were created [Col. 1:15]. This Son is at the same time the Christ—the way, the truth, and the life, without and outside of whom no one can come to the Father; the only name given under heaven, in order that we might be saved [John 14:6]. He is the head of the church in whom the Father dwells in his fullness, so the Father through Christ, having made peace through the blood of the cross, might reconcile all things to himself, be it things on earth, or things in heaven [Col. 1:18–20].

Christianity is therefore the absolute religion, the only essential, true religion. It does not grant that other religions are of almost equal worth alongside of it. It is, according to its nature, intolerant, even as the truth at all times is and must be opposed to falsehood. It will not even be satisfied by being the first of the religions, but it demands to be the only, true, full religion that includes and fulfills all that is true and good in other religions. Christ is not a man alongside of others, but the Son of Man, who by the power of the resurrection was shown to be the Son of God, according to the Spirit of holiness, and received of the Father a name above every name, so that in that name every knee should bow and every tongue confess that he is Lord, to the glory of God the Father [Rom. 1:4; Phil. 2:9–11].

In this unity is, of necessity, implied the universality of the Christian religion. While there is but one God; he is the Creator of all things [1 Cor. 8:6]. Because there is only one Mediator between God and man, he is the Savior of the whole world [1 Tim. 2:5]. And as there is only one Spirit, proceeding from the Father and the Son, he is the only guide and leader in the truth, the exclusive teacher of the church, the all-sufficient Comforter of all believers [John 14:16, 26; 16:13].

The Holy Scriptures proclaim this universality of Christianity in the clearest and most beautiful way. The Father loved the world. Therefore, he sent his only begotten Son, that whoever believes in him will not perish but have everlasting life [John 3:16]. In that Son, God has reconciled the world to himself, not imputing its sins onto it [2 Cor. 5:17–18]. Christ himself came to earth, not to condemn the world but to save it [John 3:17]. He is the Light, the Life, the Savior of the world, a reconciliation, not alone for our sins but for the whole world [1 John 2:2]. In him, all things in heaven and on earth are reconciled to God and are also gathered together into one [Col. 1:20]. The world, which was made through the Son, is also destined for the Son as its heir [Heb. 1:2]. Someday, all kingdoms will become the kingdom of our Lord and his Christ [Rev. 11:15].

This great and glorious truth has been very often denied and underappreciated. Over the course of the centuries, there have been and there still are many Christians who, to be sure, gave the gospel significance for the religious-moral life, but who also limited its influence to that, and had no conception of its value for the natural life, for family, society, and state, for science and art. Indeed, many have thought that re-creation is in hostile opposition to creation, that grace does not do anything to nature and that, therefore, the best and most Christian was the one who withdrew from the world and shut himself up in solitude.

And advocates of unbelief have gladly made use of this and proclaimed triumphantly that Christianity was hostile to all culture and, therefore, in every respect is no longer suitable for mankind in the present day. In former centuries it may have fulfilled an excellent calling, and even today it may prove to be a comfort for the sorrows of this or that depressed person. However, for mankind as a whole, Christianity is outdated and close to disappearing. Civilization, science, art, commerce, industry—these are the gods today that go before the face of man and lead him out of the house of slavery. But the gospel of Christ has served its purpose; his kingdom is not of this world and has nothing to say to this world. Indeed, the whole of religion still has some right of existence in the church and in private, but in the marketplace of life there is no longer a place for it. Religion has nothing to do with politics. In the schools of science, in the temples of art, in the council chambers of the state, the Almighty is excluded. The liberation or emancipation of the world from God and godly things persists to the end.

There is truth, which cannot be denied, in this opinion. To be sure, Jesus came to earth and assumed the natural life; but he assumed it, to deny it and to lay it down again at the cross. He was not married, did not engage in a profession in society, did not hold an office in the State. He was neither a man of science nor practitioner of art. His whole life was a sacrifice, which consummated itself in his surrender to death. He came to die. Death was the end and purpose of his life. Even as he himself testified: he came not to be served but to serve and to give his soul as a ransom for many [Mark 10:45].

And thus he did not do this only for himself, but he demands of his disciples that they should follow him and walk in his steps. Whoever does not take up the cross cannot be his disciple [Matt. 10:38]. Whoever desires to save his life shall lose it, but whoever should lose it for his sake will find it [Matt. 16:25]. Whoever loves father or mother above him is not worthy of him, but whoever leaves everything for his name will receive a hundredfold and inherit eternal life [Matt. 10:37; Mark 10:29–30]. To enter into the kingdom of heaven, the eye that causes sin must be torn out and the hand that causes sin must be cut off, for it is better to go about life maimed than having two hands and two feet and two eyes and be thrown into the fire of hell [Matt. 18:18].

Nothing can be removed from these rigorous demands of the gospel of the cross. The gospel may be for man; it is not in any respect according to man. Whoever desires to fashion it according to the spirit of the age, according to the opinions of the day, robs it of its power and experiences nothing but disappointment; if he believes, he will provide an entry point this way. For Christ has been neither a political leader nor a civil reformer; his gospel is not suitable to serve as a social program; the Scriptures are neither a legal code nor a handbook for art or science; the handling of the word is not a preaching of human wisdom; the government of the church is not dominion nor an exercising of authority; the diaconate is not an organization to solve the problem of poverty.

Christ neither came nor gave us his word for any of this. Christ is Savior—that is his name and his work, nothing else, nothing more, but also nothing less than that. His sacrifice is a propitiation for sins [1 John 2:2]. His gospel is a glad tiding of salvation. Christianity is a religion, not a philosophy.

Nevertheless, it is also complete and perfect. It is the true, pure, full religion, the restoration to a right relation with God and, therefore, also with creation. Christ is Savior, nothing else; he is that perfectly; his gospel is the power of God to salvation for everyone that believes [Rom. 1:16].

Therefore, he does not reject anyone or anything. The rich man, who thinks he has need of nothing, he sends away empty, but the poor he satisfies with good [Luke 1:53]. Christ proclaims his thrice-repeated "woe" on the Pharisees who consider their own righteousness to be sufficient [Luke 11:37–44]. However, tax collectors and sinners he invites to come to him [Luke 15:1–2]. He heals the sick. He makes the lame walk. He cleanses the lepers. He opens the eyes of the blind. He raises the dead. He lifts his hands in blessing over the children. He announces the gospel of the kingdom of God to the poor. Christ goes everywhere through the land, doing good and spreading blessings [Matt. 11:5].

In all of this, he does not consider anything strange that is human. Different from John the Baptist, Christ came eating and drinking, so that he was called a glutton and a drunk [Matt. 11:19]. He was invited to the wedding in Cana [John 2:1–12]. He accepted invitations to meals [Luke 7:36]. He forbade his disciples to fast [Matt. 9:14–15]. He portrayed the joy of the coming salvation through the parable of a marriage feast [Matt. 22]. He promised his disciples in the last night of his life that, although he would now drink no more of the fruit of the vine with them, yet one day he would drink it with them again in the kingdom of the Father [Matt. 26:29].

Christ acknowledges and respects the ordering of natural life in all areas, because he did not break down the works of the Father but only those of the devil. He pays taxes [Matt. 17:24–27]. He refuses to act as an arbitrator between two brothers quarreling about an inheritance [Luke 12:13–15]. He commands to give to Caesar that which is his [Mark 12:17]. He requires submission to those who are seated upon the seat of Moses, and forbids his disciples, even in the most frightful hour, from use of the sword [Matt. 23:1; 26:52]. He never encourages revolt. Words of love are always heard from his lips. Love your enemies. Bless those who curse you. Do well to those who hate you and pray for those who do violence to you and persecute you [Matt. 5:44].

He also loves nature with a childlike joy. He enjoys her beauty and refreshes himself in her glory. He has an open eye for the grass of the earth and the lilies of the field, for the birds of the air and the fish of the sea. He uses the vine and fig tree, the mustard seed and the grain of wheat, grape and thorn, fig and thistle, field and flock, fishing and commerce as images and parables in his teaching about the things of heaven. The whole of nature speaks to him of the Father, who is in heaven, and who makes his sun to rise on the evil and the good and causes it to rain on the just and the unjust. So little did he disapprove of all luxury that he, when Mary once anointed him with a choice perfume, did not complain with his disciples about the waste but gladly accepted the precious honor with thankfulness.

And what determines everything? Jesus indeed laid down his natural life for our sakes, but he also took it up again and rose from the dead. When he bore our sins in his flesh on the tree and thus freed the natural life from its guilt, curse, and death, he then also made it his possession again, but now reborn, spiritualized, sanctified. The bodily resurrection of Christ from the dead is the decisive proof that Christianity does not stand in opposition to anything human or natural, but God's holy will is to perfectly redeem all of creation.

Disciples of Jesus must walk in a way that is unique. Whoever wishes to follow Jesus must, to be sure, forsake everything, but he also receives back everything, thirty, sixty, and hundredfold [Luke 14:33; Matt. 13:8]. Whoever has become one with him in the likeness of his death will also be in the likeness of his resurrection [Rom. 6:5]. Whoever suffers with him is also glorified with him—not for the first time in heaven, but already beginning here on earth. For whoever believes *has* eternal life and is renewed from day to day.[1] From cross to crown, through death to life—that is the way for both Jesus and his disciples.

But this is why everything returns to them through death in the resurrection. Having died and risen with Christ, the time they remain living in the flesh they live in faith in the Son of God, who has loved them and gave himself for them. Although they are crucified to the world, they are not taken out of the world, but the Father protects them in the world from the Evil One [John 17:15]. They remain in the calling in which they are called. The Jew, who is converted to the Lord, is not required to take on the foreskin, and the Greek, who comes to faith, is not compelled to be circumcised [Acts 15:6–11]. The servant remains a servant, although he is a freeman in the Lord; and the freeborn remains free, although he becomes a servant of Christ [1 Cor. 7:21–23]. The unbelieving husband is sanctified by the wife, and the unbelieving wife is sanctified by the husband [1 Cor. 7:14].

All natural ordering remains; they are not revolutionarily overthrown but re-created through the new spirit alone. "For the kingdom of heaven is not a matter of eating and drinking but of righteousness and peace and joy in the Holy Spirit" [Rom. 14:17]. All of God's creation is good and there is nothing condemnable if it is received with thanksgiving, for it has been sanctified by the word of God and through prayer. But believers have to think about whatever is true, whatever is worthy, whatever is just, whatever is pure, whatever is lovely, whatever is truly sound [Phil. 4:8]. Besides, all is theirs because they are Christ's and Christ is God's [1 Cor. 3:21–23].

Thus godliness is beneficial toward all things, having the promise not only of the future but also of the present life. Whoever seeks first the kingdom of God and its righteousness, to them all things will be added [Matt. 6:33]. The best Christian is the best citizen. With their confession, they neither stand outside of nor in opposition to the natural life. But highly and proudly, they carry their confession into the world and everywhere plant the banner of the cross. The gospel of Christ is a joyful message for all creation—for mind and heart, for soul and body, for family and society, for science and art. For it delivers from guilt and redeems from death. "It is the power of God for salvation to everyone who believes" [Rom. 1:16].

8

The Obligation of Confession[1]

For you were bought with a price. So glorify God in your body. (1 Cor. 6:20)

Confession has its root and origin in the heart, but is itself a matter of the mouth, a work of the lips, according to its nature and character. There are many of the opinion, however, that the latter is an incidental and an arbitrary addition to confession; in any case, a superfluous good work. They know how to adorn this opinion with fine reason. Personal faith in Christ and the salvation of the soul comes to the heart, and not by means of an external work of the lips. Silent confession and quiet testifying has more worth and bears richer fruit than the speaking of great words and the using of pious terms. Jesus himself said, "Not everyone who says to me, 'Lord, Lord,' will enter the kingdom of heaven, but the one who does the will of my Father who is in heaven" [Matt. 7:21]. It is better to confess before God in private than to go around publicly selling the truth and throwing pearls before swine. The kingdom of heaven is not of this world; it comes not in outward form but is within us. People see what is before the eye, but God looks at the heart.

Against the great untruth and lie, which prevails in the confession of the mouth, this reminder of the necessity of the conversion of the heart is perfectly appropriate. An alarming hypocrisy has crept into the work of the lips. There is an orthodoxy, which is unjustly called orthodoxy, that seeks the ground for justification before God in the outward and intellectual adoption of doctrine. Works righteousness is sin, but no less evil is doctrinal righteousness, which further causes one to look down with pride in the heart at the multitude who know not the law, and yet is entirely fruitless in the works of mercy and love. Therefore, in opposition to all false orthodoxy, it is always our calling and duty to place emphasis on the heart and to provoke people to uprightness before the Lord—for false lips are an abomination to the Lord, but those who act faithfully are his pleasure [Prov. 12:22]. He takes no pleasure in a people who draw near to him with their mouths and honor him with the lips but whose hearts are held far from him [Isa. 29:13]. The heart is the first thing God requires of every person, for life flows out of it [Prov. 4:23]. To be a Christian does not consist in the speaking of great words, but that through God we do great things.

Nevertheless, this does not in the least take away the fact that Holy Scripture attaches a great worth to the testimony of the lips and that the confession of the mouth is exceedingly special. There is no other book that so boldly unmasks all hypocrisy and at the same time values so highly the significance of the word and the power of testimony as Scripture. Speaking is nothing more or less than an essential attribute of God, his eternal, unchangeable work. In speaking, the Father eternally generates out of his own essence the Son, who is the Word, the spoken and also the self-speaking Word, which in the beginning was with God and which was God [John 1:1]. Speaking in and through that word, God brings all things into existence. He preserves and rules, recreates and renews them. His speaking is doing, his word is power, he speaks and it is, he commands and it stands fast, he calls the things that are not as if they were.

In this way as well, man is created in the image of God [Gen. 1:26–28]. He receives from his Creator not only a mind and heart but also a tongue and language. Therefore, man is called not only to think and feel but also to speak and testify. His speaking must be praise, declaring the great works of God. In this manner, the angels praise him, when they stand before the throne, singing to one another: "Holy, holy, holy is the Lord of hosts; the whole earth is full of his glory!" [Isa. 6:3]. In this way, the saints praise him, when they sing the song of Moses, the servant of God, and the Song of the Lamb, saying: "Great and amazing are your deeds, O Lord God the Almighty! Just and true are your ways, O King of the nations!

Who will not fear, O Lord, and glorify your name?" [Rev. 15:3–4]. Indeed, time and again in Holy Scripture, all creation is called on to praise the name of the Lord. "Bless the Lord, all his hosts, his ministers, who do his will! Bless the Lord, all his works, in all places of his dominion. Bless the Lord, O my soul!" [Ps. 103:21–22].

In the midst of all creation that is speaking and praising, man, who has received words to express his thoughts, may not be silent. He cannot remain silent. Even his silence is counted as assent. Neutrality is as impossible for the mouth as for the heart. Whoever does not confess Christ denies him. Silence soon shifts into doubt, unbelief, and enmity. The tongue is a fire, a world of iniquity; it contaminates the whole body and sets the whole course of nature, and it is set on fire from hell; it is untamable, an uncontrollable evil, full of deadly venom. If we do not praise the Lord God, then we will curse humanity, which is made after the image of God [James 3:5–10].

Therefore, in re-creation God's purpose is that man again speaks, praises, and proclaims God's virtues. God frees the tongue no less than the heart, language as well as the thoughts. He makes man free, both soul and body, loosening his tongue and opening his lips. He fills the mouth with laughter and the lips with rejoicing [Job 8:21]. Thoughts and words also belong together and cannot be separated. The word is the mature thought, the thought that reached freedom and independence. The thoughts in the inner man are, as it were, the branches and the words are the blossoms and fruit of it, which through the mouth and lips sprout forth and come to maturity. God is the creator and former also of this fruit of lips, consisting in the sacrifice of praise.

The saints of the Old Testament also pray: "O Lord, open my lips, and my mouth will declare your praise" [Ps. 51:15]. "My mouth is filled with your praise, and with your glory all the day" [Ps. 71:8]. When God sends out his Spirit, the prayer of Moses is answered that all the people may be prophets of God [Num. 11:24]. Then sons and daughters, young and old, manservants and maidservants begin to prophesy, and everyone in their own language proclaims the great works of God [Joel 2:28–32]. Then silence is impossible. The mouth overflows with that which the heart keeps. "I will thank you in the great congregation; in the mighty throng I will praise you" [Ps. 35:18]. "I gives thanks to you, O Lord my God, with my whole heart" [Ps. 86:12]. "I will sing praise to the name of the LORD, the Most High" [Ps. 7:17]. "I will recount all of your wonderful deeds" [Ps. 9:1]. "I will sing praises to you among the nations" [Ps. 108:3]. "I will bless the LORD at all times; his praise shall continually be in my mouth" [Ps. 34:1]. "I will thank you forever" [Ps. 52:9].

God so highly values this fruit of lips, that in opposition to those who revile and slander him, the Lord prepares praise and establishes strength, even out of the mouths of children and infants [Ps. 8:2]. If the disciples keep silent, the rocks will cry out [Luke 19:40]. God demands the whole man for his service. He wills that man love him, with mind and heart, with mouth and tongue and all power [Deut. 6:5; Matt. 22:32; Luke 10:27]. When man, due to sin, holds back this glory from him, then it is he himself who through Christ gathers out of the whole world a church, which proclaims the grace of him who called it out of darkness into his marvelous light [1 Pet. 2:9]. It is God himself who calls his people to this and requires it of them, making them able and willing [Ps. 110:3]. He compels them to it through his Spirit, leading them into the truth, making them confess Jesus as the Lord, bearing witness in them of their sonship, and making them cry aloud: "Abba! Father!" [Gal. 4:6]. Because they have been purchased at great price, the price of the blood of the Son, they are called to glorify God in their body and spirit, which are God's [1 Cor. 6:20].

This duty of confessing the Lord's name rests on every believer. In confessing with the mouth, it is revealed whether we believe, whether it is our holy earnestness, whether we love God more than the friendship with the world [James 4:4]. It is the evidence of the sum total, the gauge of faith, the crown on the work of God in us. Confession with our lips returns to God again the love and faith that he, by grace through his Spirit, has produced in our hearts. It is not a hard duty, not a severe command, but a service of love that never distresses. It is a blessed privilege, a high honor. There does not exist a more glorious work for mankind than to be allowed to confess God and to proclaim his honor.

Confession is such a privilege for the individual believer and also for the church as a whole. It believes; therefore, it speaks. Throughout all of the centuries, it confesses. For friend and enemy, it gives an account of the hope which is in it [1 Pet. 3:15]. Its testimony is as the voice of many waters. It expresses its faith in meetings and religious services, in prayers and hymns, in works of mercy and gifts of love. Always and everywhere, it confesses. It is and cannot be anything other than a confessing church.

It is highly one-sided to think of the confession of the church exclusively or even principally as the written expression of its faith. Certainly, this confession gradually became necessary for the church because of errors and heresies. Likewise, when the church works in the midst of the world, it also is a glorious testimony of its faith.

Entirely without ground are different sides denying the church of Christ's right of expressing its faith in writing and of keeping watch over its perfect maintenance. For, with such a written confession, it does not condense the word of God but only explains the contents of that word according to the degree of faith and knowledge granted to it in a given time. It does not attack the authority of the Scriptures by this but solely tries to maintain this, being careful not to sacrifice Scripture to the arbitrariness of the individual. It does not bind consciences with it, but frees these from the ever emerging errors of man, striving to lead all thoughts captive to the obedience of Christ [2 Cor. 10:5]. With it, it does not cut off development but tries to keep this and to guide it down the right path, the path of building up and not breaking down. The confession of the church does not stand alongside of, much less above, but profoundly under Holy Scripture. Scripture is and remains the only, perfect, sufficient rule of faith and life.

Even if a church will not fix its faith in written form, as long as and insofar as it is a church, it will always have a confession. But when it outlines its faith in writing, from that it obtains an advantage. This advantage is that the truth, insofar as it has acknowledged it, is handed down unaltered from generation to generation and is better upheld against all adversaries. A great educational value comes to the confession of the church. The individual grows up to maturity in this confession and soon accepts it freely and independently. Just as a child in every area of life gradually enters into the work of his forefathers, so he also lives from year to year on the spiritual inheritance of the fathers.

No one begins at the beginning. Everyone stands on the shoulders of those who were before him. Every one of us lives on the treasures that parents and grandparents have gathered for them. The only requirement that comes to us is that with the utmost exertion we attain and make our own that which we have inherited from the fathers. In this way, a child also accepts the confession of the church, so that this may afterwards become the free and independent expression of his personal faith.

But also on account of this, however distinguished the written confession is, it can never be severed from personal faith, nor can it ever be torn apart from its connection to the testimonies and deeds with which the church distinguishes itself from and places itself in opposition to the world. It is not a document that binds us because of its honored antiquity. It bears no authority that is laid upon us by the distant past. But it is borne and inspired from moment to moment by the faith of the church. Thus it proceeds from generation to generation. Even in the present day, it is still our confession, and this is not because our fathers drafted it and delivered it to us. Even as it was for them in former centuries, the purest expression of our faith, the clearest explanation of the truth of God, the most beautiful exposition of the treasures of salvation that is granted to us by God in Christ, so it is also for us today.

From our youth, we are raised in the confession of the church, which we now, in faith, confess as our own.

9

The Opposition to Confession

For I would have you know, brothers, that the gospel that was preached by me is not man's gospel. (Gal. 1:11)

Confession goes against flesh and blood, against the world and Satan. Every man, by nature, is hostile to the proclamation that Jesus is the Christ. To the superficial observer, it may seem strange that the gospel has always been met with such strong opposition. Yet it is a joyful message for all creation; it speaks of nothing but grace, peace, and salvation; it demands nothing and gives everything. Yet it finds resistance and enmity everywhere; it is an offense to the Jews and foolishness to the Greeks [1 Cor. 1:23]. The gospel may be *for* man, but it is not *from* man [Gal. 1:12]. If man had invented it, it would be different; it is of divine origin and therefore is not in accordance with the thoughts and desires, with the lusts and the passions of man. Mind and heart, desire and will, soul and body rebel against the gospel of Christ. In that rebellion, man is externally supported by the whole world through the whole kingdom of darkness.

Certainly, there is a difference in the circumstances. In days of peace and rest, the opposition to the gospel is not as serious as in times when the church is oppressed and persecuted by the world. Much more courage is necessary to stand up for Christ in a godless community of sinners and scoffers than in a circle of relatives and friends who altogether confess the truth. Likewise, it takes a stronger faith to not be ashamed of the cross of Christ in a circle of nobles and scholars than among simple people in a rural town.

But, in principle, the opposition is the same everywhere. For the flesh, the world, and Satan are always the same—plus the greatest and strongest enemy who opposes the confession of Christ dwells in our own heart [Jer. 17:9; Mark 7:21–22]. The form in which the enmity occurs may vary. Nevertheless, always and everywhere the confession of the Lord's name requires a denying of ourselves and a bearing of the cross. Scorn and contempt become the part and portion of everyone, in whatever circle, who breaks with the world and follows Jesus.

Even when faith has worked in the heart and compelled a confession, there is much that constantly shuts our lips and restrains us from the free acknowledgement of Jesus' name!

Look no further than Peter who, in the hour of trouble, denied his master and even later in Antioch causes himself to be guilty of hypocrisy out of fear of the brothers of the circumcision [Mark 14:66–72; John 18:15–27; Luke 22:54–62; Gal. 2:11–21]. Yet Peter was the most prominent of the apostles, who received the name of Rock for his glorious and bold confession of Jesus' Messiahship, and who felt himself bound with such a strong love to his Savior that he would enter death with him and cast far from him the possibility of denying the Lord [Matt. 16:18; 26:33–35]. If he could fall and did fall, who then can remain standing? For whom, then, is the warning superfluous that whoever "thinks that he stands take heed lest he fall"? [1 Cor. 10:12].

The history of the Christian church in our eyes holds many beautiful examples of steadfast martyrdom, but it also contains the sad stories of thousands upon thousands who in the hour of temptation denied the faith or who drew back from the confession to crooked paths. These are the ones who have no root in themselves but endure for a while, then when tribulation or persecution arises on account of the word, the one who heard the word and received it with joy immediately falls away [Matt. 13:21; Mark 4:16–17].

The believer lies exposed to many dangers, so many cliffs upon which he is threatened to be stranded: the "desires of the flesh and the desires of the eyes and pride of life"; fear of the loss of one's name and honor, of possessions and life, each exert themselves in turn, or together to tear the disciple of Jesus from the steadfastness of his faith [1 John 2:16]. Perhaps the force that exerts the greatest power under all these trials and temptations is the so-called practice of a false sense of shame. For even when the tribulations and persecutions are over, it continues to work on and makes thousands and ten thousands to fall. In low and high society, among the rich and the poor, in the midst of the insignificant and considerable, this false sense of shame places a heavy stumbling block in the way of the confession of the Lord's Name.

There is something deeply humiliating in the fact that in the depth of our heart we are ashamed of Jesus. For he was a man who went through the country doing good and blessing, who was gentle and humble of heart, and who truly died a shameful death on a cross at the hands of his enemies who were also his judges and therefore condemned him although he was entirely and perfectly innocent [Matt. 11:29; Heb. 12:1–3; James 5:6]. There must be something wrong with us, we must be morally sick, if we are ashamed of such a man and dare not take his name upon our lips.

In general, shame is an unpleasant feeling that connects us with a certain condition or action, and as a result lowers other people's respect of us. Sometimes shame can be good. For example, after Adam violated the command of God and was ashamed of himself, he thereby showed that he felt his action to have been evil and was aware of his fall [Gen. 3:7–8]. Shame is certainly not always a fruit of faith, but it is also found with the natural man and serves as proof that man has not become an animal or a demon on account of sin, but rather that he has remained human and therefore has retained a feeling of his dignity and honor.

Nevertheless, alongside of this true and good shame, there also exists a false, wrong shame. It is found within us when we feel embarrassed about something that in itself is good but that causes others to lower their estimation of us. Therefore, we are often ashamed of the good impressions that the proclamation of the gospel has left upon us; of the accusations of our conscience; of the repentance that occurs after a sinful deed has been committed; of the tenderheartedness and sensitivity that in certain circumstances takes hold of us. On account of it we are afraid that others, noticing this, will despise and mock us; that they will consider us weak, simple, and childish; that we will lose our name as strong, brave, and courageous persons.

Now this false shame also often assaults us with respect to the gospel of the cross. We are ashamed of the church that does not consist of many wise, powerful, or noble. We are ashamed of the Bible, which is so strange and peculiar and which is rejected and contested by men of culture and science. We are ashamed of Christ, who claimed to be the only begotten Son of God, the anointed of the Father [John 3:16; Acts 10:37–38]. We are ashamed of his cross, which was a stumbling block to the Jews and folly to the Greeks [1 Cor. 1:23]. We are ashamed of the whole special revelation of God, which reveals us to ourselves and demonstrates to us our spiritual poverty.

We are afraid that by siding with Christ we will lose entirely our name and honor as a person before others and will become an object of scorn and derision, of abuse and persecution. We fear that through the confession of Christ, our dignity, personality, and humanity will be injured and suffer loss. Therefore, even in the false shame lies the foundation of a darkened understanding that we were once created in the image of God and still have a certain status and honor to preserve [Gen. 1:27]. The respect he has for himself and for others in the end makes no difference, because even in his deepest fall he remains human and continues to bear the identity of man—that is, of God's image and likeness.

But under the influence of sin, this awareness works now in the wrong direction. For it is true that by giving ourselves to Christ for salvation, we fall in our own estimation and in the estimation of others, and we lose our name and honor with other people. Nevertheless, this estimation rests upon a delusion. That name and that honor are built upon an imagination.

For by nature, we consider ourselves rich, prosperous, and in need of nothing. Yet when we embrace the gospel, we see that we are poor and blind and naked and in need of everything [Rev. 3:17]. Our honor with man is likewise also mostly the fruit of ignorance and appearance. The art of winning the hearts and praise of man consists of concealing our true nature and allowing them to form an opinion of our person according to our external learned behavior. God is true, but every man is a liar; man does not always speak falsely, but he is untrue; he is perfidious in life itself [Rom. 3:4]. Being and appearance, essence and revelation, inward and outward man, are in contradiction with each other. While the mouth occasionally overflows with love, and the face reveals nothing but friendship, out of the heart of man comes forth evil thoughts, murders, adulteries, fornication, thefts, false witness, and blasphemies [Matt. 15:19]. If the saint knew the man in his inward existence and looked into the innermost depth of his heart, he would flee from him in horror. Therefore, the love of Christ—who knew what was in man and yet sought him and gave himself unto death on his behalf—is incomparably great.

In this way, we really live with ourselves and for others in a delusion and chimera. We give up, correctly considered, essentially nothing when we believe in Christ, because we have essentially nothing. We surrender only the delusion that we live, that we are rich and prosperous, and that we lack nothing. The dreadful misery of sin consists not in that we are blind, but that we, being blind, nevertheless imagine that we can see. Sin is guilt, blemish, and shame, but it is also foolishness and absurdity.

The word of the Lord upsets that delusion of ours. We must deny that fancy if we desire to be saved by Christ. For Christians that means to count our own opinion and that of others as of no worth and worthiness, and instead to accept the judgment of God over our own and hoping only for his grace and mercy. The confession of Christ implies that we lose ourselves and everything, our name and honor, our possessions and blood, our soul and life. It is precisely against this that the false shame protests. The desire for self-preservation, in appearance, compels and drives man with all his strength and power to oppose the gospel.

"For the mind that is set on the flesh is hostile to God, for it does not submit to God's law; indeed, it cannot" [Rom. 8:7]. The natural person does not understand the things of the Spirit of God [1 Cor. 2:14]. And neither does he understand that losing one's life is the only way to truly save it [Matt. 16:25].

10

The Strength of Confession

Therefore I want you to understand that no one speaking in the Spirit of God ever says "Jesus is accursed!" and no one can say "Jesus is Lord" except in the Holy Spirit. (1 Cor. 12:3)

"What is impossible with man is possible with God" [Luke 18:27]. All our ability is from him. All genuine confessing comes from the faith of the heart, which is a gift of God, a fruit of the work of the Holy Spirit [1 Cor. 12:3; Gal. 5:22; Eph. 2:8–9].

Even though Christ had accomplished everything, it still would have been fruitless if, after his ascension to heaven, he had not sent the Holy Spirit who guides believers into all truth [John 16:13]—for the whole world stands in opposition to Christ and loves darkness rather than light [John 3:19]. But the Holy Spirit has come to testify of Christ in the midst of the world [John 15:26]. He is the only but also the almighty witness of Christ. All revile Christ, but the Holy Spirit glorifies him [John 16:14]. All condemn Christ, but the Holy Spirit justifies him [1 Tim. 3:16]. All reject Christ, but the Holy Spirit stands up for him and pleads his cause to the consciences of men. All say, "Jesus is accursed!" but the Holy Spirit says that "Jesus Christ is Lord, to the glory of God the Father" [1 Cor. 12:3; Phil. 2:11].

He bears witness to Christ in the word, which he put forward through the writings of the prophets and apostles. He bears witness to Christ in the world, which he convicts of sin, righteousness, and judgment [John 8:46]. He bears witness of Christ in the church, who confesses him to be its Lord and God. He bears witness of Christ in the heart of every believer, who through this knows that he is a child of God and cries out "Abba! Father!" [Gal. 4:6; Rom. 8:15]. Against that testimony of the Holy Spirit, nobody and nothing can stand. As soon as the Spirit of the Lord accompanies the proclamation of the word of God with his Almighty power, then the hardest heart is broken, the most stubborn knee is bowed, and the loudest mouth is stopped. In the face of his testimony, all our thoughts and considerations are of no significance; they burst like a bubble. No one speaking by the Spirit of God says, "Jesus is accursed," and everyone who has received that Spirit confesses him as his Savior and Lord [1 Cor. 12:3].

But even then, when faith has been implanted in the heart, the working of the Spirit always remains necessary, leading faith to confess in word and deed in the face of the manifold temptations to unfaithfulness—for it is God who works in us not only to will but also to do his good pleasure [Phil. 2:13]. From him, we receive both the power of faith and the boldness to confess.

That is why David prayed that God might not take his Holy Spirit from him and might strengthen him with a free and bold spirit [Ps. 51:11–12]. When Peter and John once stood before the great counsel, and afterwards when they were released, they told their brothers of their experiences and all together lifted up their voices to God, saying, "Now, Lord, look upon their threats and grant to your servants to continue to speak your word with all boldness. . . . And when they had prayed, the place in which they were gathered together was shaken, and they were all filled with the Holy Spirit and continued to speak the word of God with boldness" [Acts 4:29, 31]. Even the apostle Paul requested the prayers of the church, that words might be given to him, that he might open his mouth boldly to proclaim the mystery of the gospel [Eph. 6:19].

Above all, this boldness to speak and testify is essential for the minister of the word, but then also for every believer. It consists of the courage to give witness to the truth of God in Christ in a firm, trusting faith, openly and freely before each and every one. It is founded in the blessed awareness of the removal of guilt, in the boldness to approach the throne of grace and to ask everything of him in prayer [Heb. 4:16]. It is strengthened in us by the many examples of brave and steadfast confession, of which both Holy Scripture and history recount.

To start with, there is the example of Christ. He is in himself the word, the truth, and the perfect revelation of God [John 1; 14:6; Col. 1:15]. And he came into a world that lay in bondage to sin and deceit. His appearance alone, without a doubt, was a protest that was bound to provoke the hatred and enmity of the world [Isa. 53:2]. It could not bear Jesus. His existence was its judgment. That is why the world strained every muscle to banish this righteous one from the earth. Nevertheless, Jesus remained faithful to his Father and was obedient even to the point of death on a cross [Phil. 2:8]. Every temptation he withstood, all enmity he endured, before the Jewish Sanhedrin he verified his divine sonship, and before Pontius Pilate he made the good confession [Matt. 27:11; Mark 14:53–65; Luke 23:1–3; John 15:18; Heb. 4:15; 1 Tim. 6:13]. In this manner, Christ revealed himself to be the true and "faithful witness," "the apostle and high priest of our confession," who has left us an example that we should walk in his steps [Heb. 3:1; Rev. 1:5; 1 Pet. 2:21].

There are also the many thousands of angels into whose fellowship believers have come through Christ Jesus. They likewise exhort us to persevere in the fight—for they accompanied Christ in all his ways and ascended and descended upon the Son of Man all the days of his earthly sojourn [John 1:51]. They attend to the church in its walk through the world and are "sent out to serve for the sake of those who are to inherit salvation" [Heb. 1:14]. They long to look into the mysteries of salvation and rejoice over every sinner who repents [1 Pet. 1:12; Luke 15:10]. They are given to us as examples because of their perfect obedience, and through us the manifold wisdom of God might be made known to them [Eph. 3:10].

There is already the great cloud of witnesses that surrounds us, the whole church triumphant, whose members, although they do not observe our struggle as eyewitnesses, nevertheless encourage us and provoke us to imitate them by their example as witnesses of faith [Heb. 12:1]. They have, at least a portion of them, "suffered mocking and flogging, and even chains and imprisonment" [Heb. 11:36]. But they were not ashamed of the good confession and remained faithful to the end [Rev. 6:9–11; 7:13–17]. And their number is increasing day by day [Acts 16:5]. The spirits of the righteous made perfect presently already form a multitude no man can number, and they have been taken into heaven and are our forerunners and examples in the faithful confession of Christ [Heb. 12:23].

Finally, there is also the church militant on earth, which strengthens us by holding fast to the confession of our hope without wavering [Heb. 10:23]. Truthfully, it has been said that every Christian should believe so firmly that, although all others should fall away, he would still remain standing firm and steadfast. While this is true, as a rule man is not intended nor is he able to endure such solitude. To be sure, God can grant such grace that if we were forsaken by all, we could yet proceed upon our path with joyful courage. But generally, God keeps us standing in and through the communion of saints. For just as we in one body have many members, and these members do not all perform the same work, so also we who are many are one body in Christ are each other's members [1 Cor. 12:12]. As such, all believers have communion with the Lord Jesus and all of his treasures and gifts, and each one must feel he is obliged to use, willingly and joyfully, his gifts for the benefit and blessing of the other members [1 Pet. 4:10].

Therefore, the ones who confess Christ are never alone. Sometimes, in a certain place and at a given time, they may feel lonely and abandoned. But even then it is very often revealed that there are yet thousands who, with them, have not bowed the knee to Baal [1 Kings 18:18; Rom. 11:4]. And when out of the anguish of their souls they arise and look over all the earth and throughout the ages, from the beginning to the end of the world, they realize that they are members of a communion that is gathered in unity of faith out of the whole human race by the Son of God and by him likewise protected and preserved. The church of Christ is the essence of humanity, the salt of the earth, the light of the world [Matt. 5:13–14]. Whoever is a living member of it counts among his brothers and sisters the best and greatest and noblest of our generation, prophets and apostles, church fathers, martyrs, and reformers. And at their head stands "the faithful witness, the firstborn of the dead, and the ruler of the kings on earth" [Rev. 1:5].

At least in our country there is no reason at all to withdraw and lock ourselves up into obscurity. For Christians are nowhere and never a sect, although they are opposed and contradicted everywhere. Nevertheless, in the Netherlands, whose national existence was born out of the Reformation, Christians face very little of this. Christianity here in this land is truly national, and the ones who confess the Reformed faith are not strangers and aliens, but fellow citizens and members of the household, children of those fathers who, with their possessions and their blood, fought victoriously for truth and liberty against error and the binding of their consciences. When we remember all these things, what sort of examples ought we to be then of a faithful confession and a holy walk [2 Pet. 3:11]!

To be sure, the power of faith is necessary to row upstream and to bear all that evil men speak of us, even though it is deceitful; they do so on account of the gospel. On some, there is a bewitching influence that comes from the masses. In every circle, the danger is to submit to the great numbers and to conform ourselves to the majority.

On the other hand, however, believers can derive encouragement for themselves from the thought that they all together "have come to Mount Zion and to the city of the living God, the heavenly Jerusalem, and to innumerable angels in festal gathering, and to the assembly of the firstborn who are enrolled in heaven, and to God, the judge of all, and to the spirits of the righteous made perfect, and to Jesus, the mediator of a new covenant" [Heb. 12:22–24].

Therefore, then, we have nothing to fear, for those who are with us are more than those who are with them [2 Kings 6:16].

11

The Reward of Confession

"So everyone who acknowledges me before men, I also will acknowledge before my Father who is in heaven." (Matt. 10:32)

There is a reward attached to the faithful confession of the Lord's name, which is great in the heavens. Holy Scripture continually speaks of a reward that will be conferred to believers at the return of Christ [Matt. 5:12; 1 Cor. 3:11–15; 2 Cor. 5:10; 1 Pet. 1:3–9]. It is given as a recompense, for that which the disciples of Jesus here on earth denied themselves for his sake, or for what they suffered, or for the good works of mercy and love they completed [Eph. 2:10; Gal. 6:9–10; Heb. 13:16]. Scripture does not hesitate to encourage believers to faithfully persevere in their confession by the promise of such a reward [Luke 6:35; 2 John 1:7–8]. Scripture is not concerned that it will introduce a false element into the practice of godliness; rather, it will give rise to the exercise of virtue to serve God for the sake of heavenly salvation.

For although constantly speaking of a reward, Scripture is very strongly averse to all service for reward. The reward that awaits the faithful soldiers is not obligatory, it is not a future right that is theirs by nature, nor is it a payment due for accomplished labor. Such a reward is not known to Scripture, for it cuts it at the root of the relationship in which it places man as creature to God his Creator. Whoever has accomplished everything that was commanded of him is even then only an unprofitable servant [Luke 17:7–10]. Man is and has nothing of his own and therefore can give nothing to God, upon whom man is absolutely dependent. He can give nothing because he has to receive everything. He is not a party across from God who, as in a contract, has his own inalienable rights and can demand pay for the labor to be delivered.

Nevertheless, God for his part has, of his own free will, committed himself to richly crown all who walk in his ways with the gifts of his grace. To this end, he obligated himself in the first covenant, when he opened the way to eternal life and heavenly salvation through obedience to his commandment. This was not a reward in the sense of a wage for work performed, for what proportionality exists between the very easy keeping of the Lord's commandment—which is itself binding—and the free gift of eternal, blessed life in communion with God?

In the same way, in the covenant of grace he commits himself to give eternal life to everyone who believes in Christ. However, there is still very little room to speak of a reward in the actual sense of the word, because believing is nothing other than accepting the gift of grace that has been revealed in Christ. It is, therefore, no more deserving of reward than a castaway who upon the verge of perishing and sinking into the depths grasps the life line. Nevertheless, God is so good, not for his own sake but for Christ's sake, that he binds to faith the forgiveness of sins and life everlasting; and through this blessedness that awaits believers, he encourages them in the fight.

Therefore, both are true: that, on the one hand, connected to faith is the guaranteed possession of all the benefits of the covenant before all works; and, on the other hand, the believer is earnestly exhorted to do good works, as if all of these benefits were only to be obtained in this way. The believers are chosen from eternity, and yet they must endeavor to make their calling and election sure [2 Pet. 1:10]. Through faith, they possess eternal life, and yet one day they will receive it from the hand of the Father as a reward for their self-denial. They are branches of the vine who without Christ can do nothing and yet are exhorted to abide in him, in his word, and in his love [John 15:1–17]. They are the workmanship of God created in Christ Jesus for good works, which God prepared beforehand, and yet they must walk in them [Eph. 2:10]. They are holy and nevertheless must sanctify themselves from day to day [1 Pet. 1:15–25]. Those who are with Christ Jesus have crucified their flesh with its passions, and they are also called to put to death what is earthly in them [Gal. 5:24; Col. 3:5]. They are certain of their salvation, for God's election is immutable, his calling irrevocable, his covenant immovable, and his promises are yes and amen; yet believers are continually urged to work out their own salvation with fear and trembling, to be faithful to death, and to persevere to the end [Matt. 24:13; 2 Cor. 1:20; Phil. 2:12; Rev. 2:10].

Holy Scripture does not encourage a passive but an active Christianity. It desires that believers continually become what they are; that they acquire what they have inherited; that they more and more make themselves possessors of what, in Christ, belongs to them. That is why, on the one hand, the same thing that can be an undeserved free gift can also be, on the other hand, represented as a reward. It may be called a reward because faith and perseverance in faith are the only way that believers can participate in the benefits that in Christ are given to them out of grace alone. Without sanctification, no one will see God [Heb. 12:14].

We now understand that the reward is heavenly salvation itself, and then again, the different degrees of glory that will be granted to the believers according to their works. As it is on earth, so shall it be in heaven [Matt. 18:18]. There is diversity in unity. One is the glory of the sun, another the glory of the moon, and yet another the glory of the stars; for each star differs in glory from the next star [1 Cor. 15:41]. In the Father's house, where all the children of God dwell, there are many rooms [John 14:2]. According to the measure of their faithfulness, each church will receive from the king of the church their own jewel and crown [Isa. 62:3]. "For we must all appear before the judgment seat of Christ, so that each one may receive what is due for what he has done in the body, whether good or evil" [2 Cor. 5:10].

At this time, the separation between man and man will be completed. At the first coming of Christ—yes, already at his very first announcement in the promise—this crisis, this judgment in the world began [Gen. 3:15]. Christ has come for the resurrection and the fall of many [Luke 2:34]. He did not come to bring peace to the earth but the sword, to set a man against his father, a daughter against her mother, and the daughter-in-law against her mother-in-law [Matt. 10:34–35]. He compels all to choose for or against him [Luke 14:23]. His word is a judge of the thoughts and attitudes of the heart [Heb. 4:12]. His gospel is a fragrance of life unto life or a fragrance of death unto death [2 Cor. 2:16]. He will complete this separation on the day of his final coming when everything will be revealed before his judgment seat, for the Father has given all judgment to the Son because he is the Son of Man [John 5:22].

Whether Christ acknowledges a person to be his or not and confesses him before his Father, who is in heaven, determines everyone's lot [Matt. 10:32–33]. Our acquittal and salvation depend upon his public confession.

Christ was not ashamed of us at his incarnation. To be sure, he had many reasons to be. He himself was the firstborn of the Father, the radiance of the Father's glory and the exact image of his being—who thought it not robbery to be equal with God [John 3:16; 10:30; 17:5; Heb. 1:3; Col. 1:15; Phil. 2:6]. We were laden with guilt, unclean from head to toe, and subject to decay [Ps. 38:4; Rom. 8:20–21], yet he was not ashamed to call us his brothers [Heb. 2:11]. He was not ashamed of us before God or before the holy angels [Mark 8:38]. He took on our flesh and blood, assumed our nature, and became like us in everything apart from sin. In Christ, even God was not ashamed to be called our God [Heb. 11:16].

Therefore, he will likewise not be ashamed of us in the day of his future. To be sure, at that time he will come again not as a servant but as Lord, not to suffer but to be glorified, not to a cross but with a crown [Rev. 6:2; 19:16]. Nevertheless, he will not be ashamed of us, for the one who ascended far above the heavens is the same one who descended to the lowest parts of the earth. The one who judges is the Son of Man who once came to seek and to save the lost [Luke 19:10]. Our judge is our Savior; he never forgets nor forsakes his people [Deut. 31:6; Isa. 33:22]. "So everyone who acknowledges me before men, I also will acknowledge before my Father who is in heaven" [Matt. 10:32].

In full view of the whole world so that all of creation may hear it, he will publicly stand up for his faithful confessors. However despised they may have been in this world, Christ will take their name upon his lips and proclaim it to every ear that they are his—the ones whom he has bought with his own blood and of whom no power in the world or in hell will be able to rob him [Rom. 8:38–39].

As Christ says, so will it be. His judgment will apply to the whole of creation. His confession will concern all creation. No one will be able to criticize it. No one will dare to oppose it. His judgment will be exalted above all criticism and will stand high above the judgment of all men and devils. The heavens and the earth and hell and all creation will eternally submit to it.

Of greater importance than all of this is that the Father will rest in this work of his Son [Heb. 4:9–10]. Just as after creation God saw all that he had made and, behold, it was very good, in that way at the end of days he will look down with divine pleasure upon the great work of redemption that Christ accomplished [Gen. 1:31]. When the church without spot or wrinkle is set before him, and the perfected kingdom has been given to him, then the Father will adopt all of the redeemed of the Son as his children, inviting them to participate in his communion and enjoy his presence [Eph. 5:25–27; Rev. 21:2, 7].

The public confession on behalf of believers by Christ before his Father, who is in heaven, will be the guarantee of their eternal salvation and glory [Matt. 10:32].

12

The Triumph of Confession

Therefore God has highly exalted him and bestowed on him the name that is above every name, so that at the name of Jesus every knee should bow, in heaven and on earth and under the earth, and every tongue confess that Jesus Christ is Lord, to the glory of God the Father. (Phil. 2:9–11)

Deep in the heart of man lies buried the hope that truth will one day gain the victory over falsehood and that good will one day triumph over evil. All religions foster this expectation and speak of a victory that will be won by the kingdom of light over that of darkness at the end of time. All systems of philosophy conclude by painting an ideal state in which mankind, surrounded by the pure atmosphere and clear sunshine of the future, will dwell in peace and joy, true, free, and good. All men long for paradise, in which innocence will return and prosperity will be the portion of all. Even unbelievers surrender themselves to this sweet hope and dream of a kingdom of truth, goodness, and beauty, that after some time will spread out over the whole earth.

Nevertheless, that hope lacks sufficient ground. On what ground can people believe in a triumph of truth and righteousness, if there is no God of truth and righteousness and no Christ, whom the Father anointed to establish that kingdom and to create the new heavens and the new earth? The idols of the unbelievers are the works of the hands of men; the future expectations of philosophers are the inventions of the human brain. Truth, goodness, and beauty are pleasant sounds but are unable, within themselves, to rule over all humanity.

Whoever, therefore, expects salvation is forced to build his hope on men and look forward to them gradually and in time recognizing the truth and practicing virtue. However, because of all of this, that hope is presently extremely weak. Certainly, there is progress in material prosperity, an expansion of man's command over nature, and an ever-increasing enslavement of nature's powers to the making of a more comfortable life.

But, according to all acknowledgment, the moral progress does not keep step with the material progress. In our century, which looks down from on high upon all her predecessors, justice is trampled underfoot, righteousness stumbles on the streets, a love of and thirst for money increase, and the glorification of power knows no bounds. Culture, science, and art have even become subservient to this brutal force. There is an oversaturation of culture on the one hand and misery and lamentation on the other. Humanity appears to be farther away from paradise than ever before.

In every case, it is clearly proven by history that salvation is not to be expected, either from the exertion of human strength or from the immanent self-development of the world. If there is nothing else, then only dim despondency and anxious despair remain. Whoever is without God and without Christ is also without hope in the world [Eph. 2:12]. The kingdom of heaven was established gradually and not simply established on earth all at once; neither will it be completed in the future in this way.

Salvation and deliverance must come from above. Once again, just as it is in the natural life, so it is in the spiritual life. In the same way that the earth must receive its light and its air, its rain and sunshine, its growth and fertility from above, so also it is in mankind's spiritual life. It is dependent on the world of the invisible and eternal treasures where Christ is, seated at the right hand of God [Col. 3:1].

From above, therefore, he—who is the light, the life, and the salvation of the world—descends [John 8:12]. From above, he gathers, preserves, and protects the church, which is his body [Col. 1:18; Eph. 1:22]. Because of this, he has been exalted as head to the Father's right hand, that he should fulfill all things concerning himself, and as king he must reign until all enemies have been brought under his feet [1 Cor. 15:25; Ps. 110].

And so, he will one day descend from above [1 Thess. 1:9–10; 4:16–17]. His second coming is understood in connection with the first and necessarily flows out of it in time. His second coming is not an arbitrary addition to, but is inseparably united to his first appearance [John 14:1–3]. The work of Christ consists in saving; not in the opening of the possibility of salvation, but in the giving of salvation itself, perfectly and eternally.

His work was therefore not finished with the purchasing of salvation on earth. Of what benefit to us would a Christ be who would only die for us but not live and pray for us and be present before the face of God's for our good? Nevertheless, he who has descended is the same one who has ascended far above all heavens, that he should fulfill all things [Eph. 4:10]. What he merited, he also applies. What he began, he consummates [Phil. 1:6]. He does not rest and cannot rest until he has saved his people to the uttermost and renewed heaven and earth [Heb. 7:25; Isa. 62:6–7].

Maranatha! The Lord comes! [1 Cor. 16:21]. He comes again to reveal himself to the whole world. Revealing that he is the true, the perfect Savior. Revealing that he will save not in name but in deed and in truth. Revealing that he grants eternal life to all who have been given to him by the Father. Revealing that no one has been able to pluck or rip them out of his hand [John 10:28–29]. Revealing that he is the same yesterday, today, and forever [Heb. 13:8].

He comes again to take vengeance with a flaming fire upon all those who do not know God and who are disobedient to his gospel. Yet he also comes to be glorified in all his saints and to be admired in all who believe. He comes to be recognized and honored by all creation as the Lord, the only and true Lord, to the glory of God the Father [Phil. 2:11].

The unity of confession, accordingly, is the purpose of the history of the world.[1] One day, angels and devils and the righteous and the ungodly will agree, acknowledging that Christ is the firstborn Son of the Father and therefore the heir of all things [Heb. 1:2].

Then every knee shall bow and every tongue shall confess that Jesus Christ is the Lord [Phil. 2:10–11].

Today, that confession can be contradicted and opposed, for it holds a world of invisible things as its contents. To have insight into its truth, faith is necessary—faith being the substance of things hoped for and the evidence of things not seen [Heb. 11:1]. We walk by faith and not by sight [2 Cor. 5:7]. The world, which reckons only with things visible, can contradict the church, considering its faith foolishness and looking upon its hope as an illusion. Even this appearance is against us, for from the days that our fathers died, all things remain the same. Even from the beginning of creation all things remain the same, so that mockers can ask, "Where is the promise of his coming?" [2 Pet. 3:4].

But a change is coming. Maranatha! John had a vision:

> Then I saw heaven opened, and behold, a white horse! The one sitting on it is called Faithful and True, and in righteousness he judges and makes war. His eyes are like a flame of fire, and on his head are many diadems, and he has a name written that no one knows but himself. He is clothed in a robe dipped in blood, and the name by which he is called is The Word of God. And the armies of heaven, arrayed in fine linen, white and pure, were following him on white horses. From his mouth comes a sharp sword with which to strike down the nations, and he will rule them with a rod of iron. He will tread the winepress of the fury of the wrath of God the Almighty. On his robe and on his thigh he has a name written, King of kings and Lord of lords. [Rev. 19:11–16]

When Christ appears in glory, no one will be able to resist him. All will see him, even those who pierced him [Zech. 12:10; cf. John 19:37]. All will see him with their own bodily eyes and no unbelief, no doubt will be possible. Then all creation will have to acknowledge that Christ is the Lord. They will have to recognize it; if not freely, then compelled; if not voluntarily, then reluctantly; if not with, then against their will. From the throne in the midst of the heavens, throughout all the realms of creation, to the very depth of the great abyss, only one voice will be heard: "Christ is

Lord!" All creation together shall bow the knee before him, who was deeply humbled and died on a cross, but who is also highly exalted and seated on the throne of the universe at the Father's right hand [Phil. 2:9–10; Rom. 14:11].

What a future, what a sight! The whole of creation on its knees before Jesus! Upon all lips one, brief, recurring, foundational, all-embracing confession that is now by many scorned but will then be confessed and acknowledged by all: that Christ is the Lord to the glory of God the Father!

Come, Lord Jesus, come; yes, come quickly! [Rev. 22:20]. He who overcomes will be clothed in white raiment [Rev. 3:5]. And he, who has the seven spirits of God and the seven stars, will by no means blot his name out of the book of life, and he will confess his name before the Father and before his angels [Rev. 3:1, 5].

Epilogue[1]

Review of *The Sacrifice of Praise* by W. H. Gispen

"*The Sacrifice of Praise*" Amsterdam (1903)

The publisher Fred. H. Verschoor in The Hague has published a book from Prof. Dr. H. Bavinck that we are able to both introduce and recommend to the readers of *De Bazuin*.

The full title is *The Sacrifice of Praise: Meditations before and after Admission to the Lord's Supper*. The title is obviously taken from the words of the letter to the Hebrews 13:15: "Let us then continually offer up to God a sacrifice of praise, that is the fruit of lips that acknowledge his name." In a series of meditations, our accomplished writer covers this thought. Starting with the Covenant of Grace and the benefits that it both contains and bestows, Bavinck shows that it is the grounds or foundation of the confession, because the Covenant of Grace lies unshakably secure in the eternal mercy of God. Following this, the bringing up of children to the confession is discussed, the essence and content of the confession defined, and then the diversity and universality of the confession are brought to light. The next meditations, then, are devoted to the obligation of confession, the opposition that it encounters everywhere, the power it possesses, from its own character and nature, its practice, the reward that awaits it, and the triumph that is assured to it.

This is not a scholarly writing, but the writing is from a scholar who lays the richness of his theological knowledge, the glorious gifts of grace that have been given to him, like ripe fruit placed in the bosom of the church. It is not a dogmatic writing, but all the dogmas that are hidden in God's word, insofar as they relate directly to man's salvation and living unto God's honor, compose the bones of these meditations. And these are not the dry bones of a mounted skeleton, but rather they are bones of a living organism full of fat and marrow.

Nor is this a writing of moralism. But the purest morals, the purest way of life is proclaimed here, according to God's word. As all of God's children feel, in life they must love, that which they chase after, that they may begin, even in small ways, to live.

It is not at all a polemical or controversial writing. If Maccovius and Voetius were still alive, neither of them would have convincing objections to bring against it. It is born from the same head and heart that, some years ago, produced that beautiful and highly prized piece *The Catholicity of Christianity and the Church.*[2] Undoubtedly, these meditations will find approval and appreciation in Amsterdam and Kampen.

Therefore, we strongly insist on the general distribution of these meditations—especially at this time of the year, the so-called time of public profession of faith. It repeatedly comes to light how much misunderstanding, confusion, and, yes, even error is present in the churches with regard to confession and what is connected with the profession of faith. In fact, this is the case not only among the members of the church. Under God's blessing, this writing by Prof. Dr. Bavinck can contribute much to healthy doctrine, which is after godliness. To put it another way, this writing can help the reader to seek and love more earnestly. Now let the wealthy distribute these reflections on a large scale, to ensure that they are found in every home where young children are, and also let no pastor be lacking. They are also printed on such sturdy paper and with such a bold font that their fate is evident from that.

We have in *De Bauzin* announced books and writings we would not have dared to say with a clear conscience that we had read from the beginning to the end. We can, however, assert this about *The Sacrifice of Praise*. We have read with increasing interest and enjoyment, with complete approval and at every turn admiration, on account of the richness of thought, the clarity of argument and presentation, the pure simplicity, and sweetness of style, with thankfulness to God and to the author for this precious gift. *The Sacrifice of Praise* gave us the impression of a spring flower in the midst of the sharp, cold, fierce, spring winds; Elim in the desert of daily worries, hardships, quarrels, and murmurings.[3]

May the Lord God grant that it is the forerunner of a beautiful, refreshing, abundantly fruit-bearing summer.

W. H. Gispen

Bibliography

Barth, Karl. *Göttingen Dogmatics: Instructions in the Christian Religion*. Vol. 1. Grand Rapids: Eerdmans, 1991.

Bavinck, Herman. *Certainty of Faith*. Translated by Harry der Nederlanden. Ontario: Paideia Press, 1980.

———. "Common Grace." Translated by Raymond C. Van Leeuwen. *Calvin Theological Journal* 24, no. 1 (1989): 35–65.

———. "Confessie en Dogmatiek." *Theologische Studiën* 9 (1891): 258–75.

———. *De Zekerheid de Geloofs*. Kampen: J. H. Kok, 1901.

———. "The Pros and Cons of a Dogmatic System." Translated by Nelson D. Kloosterman. *The Bavinck Review* 5 (2014): 90–103.

———. *Reformed Dogmatics*. Edited by John Bolt. Translated by John Vriend. 4 vols. Grand Rapids: Baker Academic, 2003–08.

———. *Roeping en Wedergeboorte*. Kampen: G. Ph. Zalsmann, 1903.

———. *Saved by Grace: The Holy Spirit's Work in Calling and Regeneration*. Edited by J. Mark Beach. Translated by Nelson D. Kloosterman. Grand Rapids: Reformation Heritage Books, 2008.

Beach, J. Mark. "Introductory Essay." In *Saved by Grace: The Holy Spirit's Work in Calling and Regeneration*, ix-lvi. Grand Rapids: Reformation Heritage Books, 2008.

Bouma, Hendrick. *Secession, Doleantie, and Union: 1834–1892*. Translated by Theodore Plantinga. Neerlandia, Alberta: Inheritance Publications, 1995.

Bratt, James D. *Dutch Calvinism in Modern America: A History of a Conservative Subculture*. Grand Rapids: Eerdmans, 1984.

Brock, Cory. "Orthodox yet Modern: Herman Bavinck's Appropriation of Schleiermacher." PhD diss., University of Edinburgh, 2017.

Clement of Alexandria. *Clemens Alexandrinus erster band Protrepticus und Paedagogus*. Edited by Otto Stählin. Leipzig: J. C. Hinrichs'sche Buchhandlung, 1905.

Eglinton, James. "Dutch Inspiration for Tim Keller." Translated by Nelson Kloosterman. Accessed June 8, 2019, https://bavinck institute.org/2011/07/tim-keller-on-kuypers-and-bavincks-influence.

———. "Nederlandse inspiratie voor Tim Keller." *Nederlands Dagbald* (July 11, 2011). Accessed June 28, 2019, https://www.nd.nl/nieuws/geloof/nederlandse-inspiratie-voor-tim-keller.244786.lynkx.

———. *Trinity and Organism: Toward a New Reading of Herman Bavinck's Organic Motif*. T&T Clark Studies in Systematic Theology. London: T&T Clark, 2012.

The Encyclical Epistle of the Church at Smyrna: Concerning the Martyrdom of the Holy Polycarp (*ANF* 1:41).

Harinck, George. "Herman Bavinck and Geerhardus Vos." *Calvin Theological Journal* 45 (2010).

Harinck, George, and Lodewijk Winkeler. "The Nineteenth Century." In *Handbook of Dutch Church History*, edited by Herman J. Selderhuis, translated by Todd Rester and Jim West, 435–520. Göttingen: Vandenhoeck & Rupretch, 2015.

Kromminga, D. H. *The Christian Reformed Tradition: from the Reformation to the Present*. Grand Rapids: Eerdmans, 1943.

Kuyper, Abraham. *De Leer der Verbonden*. Amsterdam: J. H. Kruyt, 1885.

———. *E Voto Dordraceno. Toelichting op den Heidelbergschen Catechismus*. Amsterdam: JA Wormser, 1892–95.

———. *Voor een Distel een Mirt: Geestelijke Overdenkingen bij den Heiligen Doop, het Doen van Belijdenis en het Toegaan tot het Heilig Avondmaal*. Amsterdam: Höveker & Wormser, 1891.

Lecerf, Auguste. *Introduction à la Dogmatique Réformée*. Paris: Editions Je Sers, 1931.

Ralston, Joshua. "Editorial." *International Journal of Systematic Theology* 18, no. 3 (2016): 255–58.

Schaver, J. L. "The Conclusions of Synod Utrecht (1905.)" In *The Polity of Churches*, 2 vols. 3rd.ed. 2.34–37. Chicago: Church Polity Press, 1947.

Selderhuis, Herman J., ed. *Handbook of Dutch Church History*. Translated by Todd Rester and Jim West. Göttingen: Vandenhoeck & Rupretch, 2015.

Van Til, Cornelius. *An Introduction to Systematic Theology: Prolegomena and the Doctrines of Revelation, Scripture, and God*. 2nd ed. Edited by William Edgar. Phillipsburg, NJ: P&R, 2007.

Venema, Cornelius P. *Christ and Covenant Theology: Essays on Election, Republication, and the Covenants*. Phillipsburg, NJ: P&R, 2017.

Visser, John. "Karl Barth's Appreciative Use of Herman Bavinck's *Reformed Dogmatics*." *Calvin Theological Journal* 45, no. 1 (2010): 79–86.

Notes

Introduction

1. *The Encyclical Epistle of the Church at Smyrna: Concerning the Martyrdom of the Holy Polycarp* (*ANF* 1:41).

2. For example, Dolfin muted language of "consciousness," a modern philosophical/theological concept brought into modern theology from modern psychological thought, and language of "feeling," particularly, "the feeling of absolute dependence," which traces its introduction theologically to nineteenth-century German Romantic thought.

3. John Visser, "Karl Barth's Appreciative Use of Herman Bavinck's *Reformed Dogmatics*," *Calvin Theological Journal* 45, no. 1 (2010): 79–86, 79, 83. Karl Barth, *Göttingen Dogmatics: Instructions in the Christian Religion*, Vol. 1 (Grand Rapids: Eerdmans, 1991), 97.

4. Cornelius Van Til, *An Introduction to Systematic Theology: Prolegomena and the Doctrines of Revelation, Scripture, and God*, ed. William Edgar, 2nd ed. (Phillipsburg, NJ: P&R, 2007), 89.

5. Auguste Lecerf, *Introduction à la Dogmatique Réformée* (Paris: Editions Je Sers, 1931), 9.

6. Cory Brock, "Orthodox yet Modern: Herman Bavinck's Appropriation of Schleiermacher" (PhD diss., University of Edinburgh, 2017), 253; Joshua Ralston, "Editorial," *International Journal of Systematic Theology* 18, no. 3 (2016): 255–58, 257. When Josh Ralston placed Bavinck among theologians such as Barth and Schleiermacher, Cory Brock considered this a "remarkable" move. Brock goes on to say, "Bavinck now takes his place in the community of modern Reformed theologians as the choice between titans, *between the two*: Schleiermacher and Barth. Indeed, Bavinck speaks today" (Brock 253). It is plain that Bavinck's recognition as a noteworthy theologian

has come to the forefront of theological discussions in the theological world.

7. James Eglinton, "Nederlandse inspiratie voor Tim Keller," *Nederlands Dagbald*, July 11, 2011, accessed June 28, 2019, https://www.nd.nl/nieuws/geloof/nederlandse-inspiratie-voor-tim-keller.244786.lynkx. "Dutch Inspiration for Tim Keller," trans. Nelson Kloosterman, accessed June 28, 2019, https://bavinckinstitute.org/2011/07/tim-keller-on-kuypers-and-bavincks-influence.

8. Bavinck, "The Pros and Cons of a Dogmatic System," trans. Nelson D. Kloosterman, *The Bavinck Review* 5 (2014): 90–103.

9. Bavinck, "The Pros and Cons," 94, 98.

10. Bavinck, "The Pros and Cons," 94.

11. Bavinck, "Confessie en Dogmatiek," *Theologische Studiën* 9 (1891): 258–75. Here, Bavinck comments positively on Daubanton's assessment of the nature of the theological task. "Dr. Daubanton rightly demonstrates the ecclesiastical and confessional nature of dogmatics."

12. Bavinck, "Confessie en Dogmatiek," 263. The word translated as "nickname" is *bijnaam* in the Dutch, which can refer to individuals or groups. Here, Bavinck seems to be referring to the nicknames of different Christian traditions, such as Lutheran, Reformed, or Baptist.

13. Bavinck, "Confessie en Dogmatiek," 267.

14. Bavinck also published the second edition of *De Welsprekenheid (Eloquence)* in 1901 with Fred H. Verschoor.

15. Archive of Herman Bavinck, number 16 'Dakboekjes', entry on March 19 and 30th, 1873. "19 March 1873. Confession of faith made to Rev. Dosker in the Chr. Geref. Church in Zwolle." Dutch: "19 March 1873. Belijdenis des geloofs afgelegd bij Ds. Dosker in de Chr. Geref. Kerk te zwolle. "30 March 1873. Sunday confirmed by Rev. Dosker." Dutch: 30 March 1873. Zondag Bevestigd door Ds. Dosker."

16. Archive of Herman Bavinck, number 16 'Dakboekjes', entry on October 10, 1875. Dutch: "Ds. Donner sprak over Ps. 34:9. Het as Avondmaal. Voor 't eerst in mijn level sprak ik aan de tafel des Heeren de openlijke belijdenis uit, dat ik dood ben in zonden en mis daden, maar mijne eenige hope op de gerechtigheid van Christus is. O, moge ik mij niet een oordeel gegeten en gedronken hebben! Laat, O God, de wensch om u te dienen, bij mij een waarchtige geweest zijn end us onberouwelijke!"

17. George Harinck, "Herman Bavinck and Geerhardus Vos," *Calvin Theological Journal* 45 (2010), 18.

18. See D. H. Kromminga, *The Christian Reformed Tradition: from the Reformation to the Present* (Grand Rapids: Eerdmans, 1943); James D. Bratt, *Dutch Calvinism in Modern America: A History of a Conservative Subculture* (Grand Rapids: Eerdmans, 1984); Hendrick Bouma, *Secession, Doleantie, and Union: 1834–1892*, trans. Theodore Plantinga (Neerlandia, Alberta: Inheritance Publications, 1995); J. Mark Beach, "Introductory Essay," in *Saved by Grace: The Holy Spirit's Work in Calling and Regeneration* (Grand Rapids: Reformation Heritage, 2008), ix-lvi; *Handbook of Dutch Church History*, ed. Herman J. Selderhuis, trans. Todd Rester and Jim West (Göttingen: Vandenhoeck & Rupretch, 2015).

19. Harinck and Winkeler, "The Nineteenth Century," 460.

20. Beach, "Introductory Essay," xiii.

21. Harinck and Winkeler, "The Nineteenth Century," 461.

22. They were called "the Grieving ones" because they did not want to leave the state church but were forced out. Harinck and Winkeler, "The Nineteenth Century," 492–93.

23. Beach, "Introductory Essay," xiii.

24. Harinck and Winkeler, "The Nineteenth Century," 492.

25. Harinck and Winkeler, "The Nineteenth Century," 492–93.

26. Harinck and Winkeler, "The Nineteenth Century," 495.

27. Beach, "Introductory Essay," xiv.

28. Herman Bavinck, *Roeping en Wedergeboorte* (Kampen: G. Ph. Zalsmann, 1903). English: Herman Bavinck, *Saved by Grace: The Holy Spirit's Work in Calling and Regeneration*, ed. J. Mark Beach, trans. Nelson D. Kloosterman (Grand Rapids: Reformation Heritage, 2008).

29. Herman Bavinck, *Reformed Dogmatics*, ed. John Bolt, trans. John Vriend, 4 vols. (Grand Rapids: Baker Academic, 2003–08). For insight into Bavinck's thoughts on these two terms, see Bavinck's section on the "Divine Counsel" in his *Reformed Dogmatics*, vol. 2, 337–405. Both terms are a response to the question of when God decreed the elect. Did God decree this before (*supra*) or after (*infra*) the Fall (*laps*)? To put it differently, supralapsarianism traditionally argues that God decreed whom he would redeem as his own prior to his decree to permit the Fall. Alternatively, infralapsarianism argues that God determined the elect after he decreed that all men would fall in Adam.

30. Beach, "Introductory Essay," xv.

31. Cornelius P. Venema, *Christ and Covenant Theology: Essays on Election, Republication, and the Covenants* (Phillipsburg: P&R Publishing, 2017), 193.

32. Kuyper's original position on presumptive regeneration can be found in *De Leer der Verbonden* (Amsterdam: J. H. Kruyt, 1885). However, over the course of a decade, he changed his position and advocated for "assumed" or "presumptive" regeneration. Kuyper first indicates this change in *De Bauzin*, November 15, 1895. His full abandonment of the historic Reformed understanding of the relationship between baptism and the regeneration is found in his four-volume *E Voto Dordraceno. Toelichting op den Heidelbergschen Catechismus* (Amsterdam: J. A. Wormser, 1892–95), and in his devotional work *Voor een Distel een Mirt: Geestelijke Overdenkingen bij den Heiligen Doop, het Doen van Belijdenis en het Toegaan tot het Heilig Avondmaal* (Amsterdam: Höveker & Wormser, 1891).

33. Beach, "Introductory Essay," xxvii.

34. Kuyper, *E Voto Dordraceno*, III, 12. Original Dutch: "Wist ge nu zeker, dit mijn kind is een uitverkorene en God heeft het zaad der wedergeboorte reeds in dit kind op verborgene wijze gewrocht, dan natuurlijk zoudt ge uw kind den Heiligen Doop niet onthouden mogen; en op dien grond nu is het uw plicht, voorzooveel ge in het Verbond left, elk uwer kinderen, die u geboren worden, in de onderstelling dat het genadewerk Gods reeds in hen plaats greep, in den Naam van God Drieëenig te laten doopen."

35. Bavinck, *Saved by Grace*, 68–69.

36. Bavinck, *Reformed Dogmatics*, 4:525.

37. Bavinck, *Reformed Dogmatics*, 4:531.

38. Bavinck, *Saved by Grace*, 92–94.

39. J. L. Schaver, "The Conclusions of Synod Utrecht (1905)," in *The Polity of Churches*, 2 vols., 3rd ed. (Chicago: Church Polity Press, 1947), 2.34–37.

40. In 1901, Bavinck also wrote *De Zekerheid de Geloofs* (English: *Certainty of Faith*, trans. Harry der Nederlanden [Paideia Press: Ontario, 1980]); and in 1903, *Roeping en Wedergeboorte* (English: *Saved by Grace: The Holy Spirit's Work in Calling and Regeneration*, ed. J. Mark Beach, trans. Nelson D. Kloosterman [Grand Rapids: Reformation Heritage, 2008]). Both of these works are written at the popu-

lar level and, to various extents, concern the place of faith, covenant, repentance, and grace.

Chapter 1

1. Bavinck here is discussing theological covenants in distinction to biblical covenants. Historically, theologians have identified three theological covenants: the Covenant of Redemption (an intra-trinitarian covenant before time), the Covenant of Works (which Bavinck lays out in this paragraph), and the Covenant of Grace (which he will explore below). The biblical covenants are the Covenant with Noah, the Covenant with Abraham, the Covenant at Sinai, the Covenant with David, and the New Covenant. While not mutually exclusive, it is important to establish the difference.

2. For an expansion of the "organic" idea in Bavinck, see James Eglinton, *Trinity and Organism: Toward a New Reading of Herman Bavinck's Organic Motif*, T&T Clark Studies in Systematic Theology (London: T&T Clark, 2012).

3. In the earliest editions of *The Sacrifice of Praise*, "with our money and possessions" is found but was removed in later revisions.

4. See Bavinck, "Common Grace," trans. Raymond C. Van Leeuwen, *Calvin Theological Journal* 24, no. 1 (1989): 35–65.

5. Original Dutch: "Buiten bewustzijn en wil worden wij in eene wereld geplaatst, die met rijke goederen is vervuld, en gaan wij in tot de machtige erfenis der voorgeslachten; wij staan op hunne schouderen en genieten van wat zij in het zweet des aanschijns hebben verworven en saamgebracht."

Chapter 2

1. Original Dutch: "De opvoeding tot de belijdenis." A literal translation of the title of this chapter is somewhat ambiguous as "Bringing up unto Confession" and should be understood as having the sense of "training a child in the confession of faith."

2. It is interesting to note how election and covenant grasp Bavinck's "organic" ideal as one in which the whole and the parts are simultaneously considered.

3. Clement of Alexandria, *Clemens Alexandrinus erster band Protrepticus und Paedagogus*, ed. Otto Stählin (Leipzig: J. C. Hinrichs'sche Buchhandlung, 1905), 273.

Chapter 4

1. Bavinck may have in mind here "Lord's Day 64" from the Heidelberg Catechism:

> Q: "But does not this doctrine make men careless and profane?
> A: By no means: for it is impossible that those, who are implanted into Christ by a true faith, should not bring forth fruits of thankfulness."

Chapter 5

1. The penitential psalms are the seven psalms chosen by the church as liturgical prayers on days of penance and sorrow (Pss. 6, 31, 37, 50, 101, 129, and 142).

2. Heidelberg Catechism "Lord's Day 1":

> Q: What is your only comfort in life and death?
> A: That I am not my own, but belong with body and soul both in life and in death, to my faithful Savior Jesus Christ. He has fully paid for all my sins with his precious blood, and has set me free from all the power of the devil. He also preserves me in such a way that without the will of my heavenly Father not a hair can fall from my head; indeed, all things must work together for my salvation. Therefore, by his Holy Spirit he also assures me of eternal life and makes me heartily willing and ready from now on to live for him.

3. Bavinck blends these two passages together.

4. The "twelve articles" was a common way of referring to the Apostles' Creed.

Chapter 7

1. Italics original.

Chapter 8

1. The Dutch title of this chapter is "De plicht tot belijdenis." While a literal translation would render this as "The Obligation *to* Confession," the concept behind this (as the chapter demonstrates) is "The Obligation *of* Confession."

Chapter 12

1. This is the climax of Bavinck's point on confession. Previously, he had emphasized the diversity of confession (ch. 6) and the universality of confession (ch. 7). Here, however, he highlights the coming together of all confessions under the one confession that Jesus is Lord.

Epilogue

1. The epilogue is a translation of Dr. Willem Hendrick Gispen's review of the first edition of Herman Bavinck's *The Sacrifice of Praise*. The original review ran in *De Bauzin* 49, no. 12 (1903), 3.

2. Bavinck, *De Katholiciteit van Christendom en Kerk* (Kampen: Zalsman, 1888). This address was given in Kampen at the Theological School on December 18, 1888. It can be found in English as "The Catholicity of Christianity and the Church," trans. John Bolt, *Calvin Theological Journal* 27 (1992): 220–51.

3. Elim is an oasis in the Bible (see Exod. 15:27; Num. 33:9).

Subject Index

About the Editors

Cameron Clausing is a PhD candidate at the University of Edinburgh in systematic theology and a graduate of Reformed Theological Seminary and Moody Bible Institute. He is currently a visiting assistant professor of theology at Covenant College in Lookout Mountain, Georgia.

Gregory Parker Jr. is a PhD candidate at the University of Edinburgh in systematic theology and a graduate of Gordon-Conwell Theological Seminary and Cairn University. He is under care in the Presbyterian Church of America.